Letters to Betty at 80

Reflections on Authentic, Wise, and Eccentric Years

Mary Bub

Praise for *Letters to Betty at 80*

"Through daily letters to an imaginary friend, the author invites us to join her on a journey of self–discovery at age eighty. The thought provoking questions after each letter encourage the reader to go even deeper with reflection.

Letters to Betty at 80 *is a gift to women of any age who wish to discover or rediscover their true self."*

–Joan Christensen

"As I enter my eighth decade, I am grateful that I had the opportunity to read Mary Bub's book, Letters to Betty at 80. *Not only was it an honest reflection of the author's ability to share her thoughts and feelings, it provided an avenue for me to explore my own thoughts and feelings about the aging process. The questions that were posed at the end of each letter were a catalyst for me to explore my feelings about becoming an octogenarian."*

–Rita Lichterman

CONTENTS

Foreword   1

Author's Note   3

Dedication   7

Prologue   9

April   11

A Monumental Birthday

A Delightful Surprise

If I Look, Will I See? If I See, Will I Act?

Oh, the Roles We Play on the Stage of Our Life

Transitions

Angst

Great-Grandparenting

Job Descriptions

Calm and Content

Becoming Elder

Transferring

Is Any Age a New Age?

Out with the Youngers

A Shared Journey

Weddings With the Olders is Fun

Could Do Without the Ride
Music Can Soothe the Soul

May   49
Excuses
Tidal Waves
Perspective
A Soft Chair
Aunties
Mother's Day
Not So Crazy
Pocketbooks
Sister Aunties
Stalwarts
To Plan or Not
Role Models
Herding Sheep
Sanctuary
Contradictions
Choosing Our Memories
Planting Will Never be the Same
Rainy Days
Scattered Ashes
Being and Doing
Slow or Fast
A Little Fantasy

June   93
Let's Be Emotional
Acceptance is the Bane of Aging

Energy and Expectations
Tears
Poor Me
Out of the Cocoon
In Defense of Selfing
Energy Meets Expectations
Presence, Awareness, and Identity
Just an Ordinary Day
Bits and Pieces of My Heart
Voices
Destination Unknown
Raised Eyebrows
Stay the Course
Rear-View Mirror
Hoping and Wishing
Morbs
Do-Overs
Upside-Down Cake
A Quiet Mind
Signs and Wonders
The Far Reaches of My Absent Mind
Prescription for Aging

July   139
Life is a Scrabble
Independent
A Page Turned
A Little Silliness Soothes the Soul
The Party is Over

History Repeats Itself
Clock Work
Dying Has Given Me Purpose
If Wishes Were Horses
Never Stop Seeking
Magic Happens When It Happens
The Empty Chair
Settle
At a Loss Today
GONE
Yes and No
Roses Amongst the Garlic

August 173
Is There Grace in Solitude?
Round Peg in a Square Hole
80 is Just a Number
Old Hat
Enough Already
Perspective at 80
Envy
Tired
Prayer
The Waters Fine
Backsliding
Urgency
Picture Perfect
Days of Glory
Calendar Pages

Scary New Adventures
Day Off
Control What?
Going Slow or Not
Is That All There Is?
Just Thank You Will do
Sweet Tomorrow
A Little Joy
Living Wholistically
A Big and Empty House
Toss and Turn

September   227
Labor
Reality Check
Perspective
The Widow
Sailing
Tottering
Absent-Minded
Faith vs. Works
Hurrying
A New Kind of Fear
Can't - Can
Clearly
In Bed
Self-Talk and Talking to Myself
Feelings - Unnamed - Unrecognized
Intimacy

The Intuition Muscle
What Was I Thinking?
Oops!
Effort
Going Back
Metaphors
World Keeps Spinning

October 273
Highs & Lows
Marathon or Sprint
Zippers, Buttons, and Necklaces
Quiet Day
Wisdom
Words
Emotional Noise
Docile vs. Bad Ass
Self-Assured vs. Self-confident
Long Shadows
Last Kid on the Playground
When?
Feeble, Fragile, Wrinkled, Not Me
Quiet Turns to Noise
Life Keeps Rewinding at 80
Routine
Wanderlust
The Sun will Rise
Waste a Day
View Master

November 315
 Personality
 Not OK
 Never Stop Becoming
 I'm Back
 Taking the By-Pass
 Flexible vs. Spontaneous
 Gratitude Not Cliché
 Ties That Bind
 Gift to Be Simple
 Blessed or Bereft?
 Wisdom? Maybe
 What Was and What Is
 Things I Wish I Would Have
 Naked
 Message From a Hawk

December 347
 Celebrations at 80
 Stories Tumble Out
 Pumpkin Bars
 Small
 Up-Ended
 Usual
 Soon 81
 Feeling AWE
 Holidays at 80
 Winter Fog
 Fog Continued

Reality Check Again

January   373
    Finding Words
    Talking Mad
    Counting
    Amazed
    Be Holy
    Who Knew?
    Shoes
    Eighty–One

Afterword   389
About the Author   391

FOREWORD

Letters to Betty at 80 was written for anyone at eighty. I especially like the references to the author's family and the way each letter is a complete statement.

Here is a woman of wisdom who is willing to share that wisdom without being pushy or boastful about it.

I treasure my decades–long friendship with the author because she welcomes everyone as valuable. She sees my gifts and helps me recognize the gifts in everyone around me.

Carolyn Heidemann

Author's Note

Yesterday I decided by a graced moment that it was time to change the focus when writing to Betty. Betty has been a faithful companion to me through my personal grief journey. She is my alter ego and so I will continue to journey with her now as I process my eightieth year. It was not easy leaving the time spent with Betty sorting out my grief process. It was a safe space and she was a comfortable listener. I am sure that she will continue to be a great companion. The grief of losing a partner or anyone who has claimed a piece of your heart is never over. It is a place that can be visited from time to time to remind one of the most precious moments in a life shared. As we reach an age that suggests some time for reflection we, I think, find other moments or challenges in our lives that continue to be incredible moments in time.

When I reached my sixtieth birthday I wanted to celebrate the beginning of my "journey" into what I had heard was the third life stage. Many years before this turning event I had an experience of belonging to a circle of women who called themselves Bethany. During that time I was asked the familiar question,

"What attitudes or characteristics do you want to achieve in your becoming?" Now, isn't that an ethereal question? Well, I chose authentic, eccentric, and wise. Those three words have traveled with me from my sixtieth birthday until this very day. They help me center when I start to wobble. They give me direction and purpose. They even help me retain my sense of humor.

Two things that I want to share with you were very important to my grief journey. One was the use of my grief box. An imaginary box in which I stored my emotions. The other was a lesson I learned was just how important doing the ordinary things of life can be.

Recently I was visited by a memory of my mom's fiftieth birthday party. I thought, "Wow, my mom is getting really old." Now since my own fiftieth birthday is long past, I realize how radically our perception changes as we enter our own aging, checking off the years, sometimes with joy and sometimes with regret.

I don't know where this endeavor will lead as I continue to write to Betty. Although I am open to learning not only about the aging process, but more about myself, personally and as a part of my family and my relationship to others and the world around me. I hope that you will take this journey with me, and maybe even find your own "Betty".

Who would have thought that I would publish not only one book but three at the ripe old age of eighty. It is with deep gratitude that I acknowledge Elizabeth Hill and Green Heart Living Press. It would not have happened without their sincere encouragement, patience and amazing creativity. I am so thankful.

"I am pieces of all the places I have been, and the people I have loved. I've been stitched together by song lyrics, book quotes, adventure, late night conversations, moonlight and the smell of coffee."–Brooke Hampton

As I begin to write my letters to Betty, I am sure that many of the pieces of my life will appear. I look forward to sharing them with you.

Even though I still shudder a bit when saying, "I am eighty," ready, set, here we go!

Alice

DEDICATION

This book is dedicated to Alice. I met Alice while on vacation visiting a friend in Arizona. We were spending the day at a conference center. I was enjoying one of my interests, taking photographs. Sitting there on a small stone wall was a woman who appeared to me as unusual, friendly, and an interesting photo study. I didn't want to be rude and just take her photo but I was a bit timid about asking her if she would mind.

I was waiting for my friend, so I just waited. Still, I couldn't get the want in me to take the picture. Finally, I approached her and asked her if she would mind if I took her picture. "Of course not," she replied. I said that I had been wanting to ask for some time but was too timid. Her answer is why I am dedicating this book to her, she said, "Never be afraid to ask." Four words that have stayed with me for many years. A lesson from a kind, thoughtful woman, and I think a wise woman.

Thanks Alice.

PROLOGUE

Another Year

January 3, 2024

Dear Betty,

Eighty is standing in the space of what is and looking down the long road of what will be.

Another turn of the calendar year. Celebrations, anticipation, hopes and dreams and finally the crystal ball drops, cheers ring out, a new year is upon us. Still Betty, I got up this morning and all of the daily chores were still waiting for me. The coffee didn't taste any different, not any better, but not bad either. I look out of the window and it is still winter. The trees are still barren, the garden lies fallow.

How should I feel about facing another year? Ah yes, I must remember to write the correct year on my checks. Betty, I still use checks even if I have given in to learning how to pay bills online. I cannot help but wonder what this year will bring. What new challenge will come knocking on my door?

I think that I will try my best to stay in the "today" of my ongoing life, and know that tomorrow will be another today. Maybe this is the way of life in the eighties or even in the sixties, seventies. Actually, Betty, I do not think it would be bad for a person of any age to focus on living the best of their day. I guess I am feeling a bit philosophical on this today. Enough already.

Tomorrow,

Me

How do you feel about the turning of the calendar to a new year?

What new challenges do you think will come knocking on your door?

A Monumental Birthday

April 6, 2024

Dear Betty,

I woke up on the morning of my birthday (January 18, 1944). I said to myself, "It is my birthday and I am eighty years old today." Funny, I don't feel any different. What does eighty feel like? What will eighty be like? At that moment entering my eightieth year just seemed surreal. Can this really be happening?

Of course, you know, Betty, you cannot stop it from happening. Time just keeps marching on. While I was in the wake of my new reality, I was also in the early stages of grief. My husband Don died in September. My awakening also reminded me that he was not here to celebrate my birthday with me. He was not with us for Thanksgiving or Christmas and he wouldn't be with us for grandson Nik's wedding either.

It is three months later and some days I feel like I have whiplash. So many feelings have surfaced, so many memories, so many thoughts to sort out. Betty, you have been more than helpful. Now I feel as though I can move on to spending some time with issues and questions that have surfaced. I want our eightieth year together to be fruitful for myself and for anyone else who may someday come across our letters and read them with an open heart.

Soon,

Me

How do you feel when you think about being in your sixties, seventies and beyond?

What do you think would make your eighties and beyond fruitful?

What did seventy feel like? Do you feel different now?

A Delightful Surprise

April 7, 2024

Good morning, Betty,

Yesterday I had a delightful surprise. Two friends who are visiting from the east stopped in for a visit. It was some of the best conversation I have had in a long time. Yes, we talked a little about their move out east and the changes that they have encountered but mostly we talked about my grief journey. They listened with interest. They made me feel that I had something to share. That my grief journey has meaning and that I have something to give and to receive.

Coffee this morning brought me to thinking about a book that I have been listening to each night before I go to bed. Maybe that is why the story stays with me through coffee time. Anyway, it is called *The Last Word in the Dictionary* by Pip Williams.

I guess I might call myself a word junky. The word that came out of the book is "morbs": a person afflicted with temporary melancholy or sadness. I made a copy of it and gave it to each of my daughters. Now we have a way of saying how we are feeling without going into a ton of explanations. However, today I am not suffering from the morbs.

OK,

Me

Have you found new words to explain your feelings at this stage of your life?

How do you think about words and their meanings as they relate to how you might process your life journey?

If I Look, Will I See? If I See, Will I Act?

April 8, 2024

Dear Betty,

Today is the day of the total eclipse. I am sure that I could spew out several metaphors about this but I have decided not to. I want to play with something different today. I have been collecting words that help me describe my eightieth year day by day. I am going to attempt putting them into letters to you in the hopes that they will be helpful in discerning this new journey.

The word for today is observer. I am not sure that I have taken on this new role because being together with friends and family at social gatherings is different because Don is not with me, or if it is part of the aging process. I notice that I like the observer role. I find it interesting to watch and observe the family dynamics, the kind of conversations held and of course the interaction with the little ones.

Being an observer can be a reflective state to be in. On the other hand, it can also open doors to behaviors that I am not so sure I want to process now. So far, since it is really just four months into my year, being an observer has given me a new context to use as a guidebook as I learn, experience and create this adventure. I find that

I can choose how I want to act or interact when I see a behavior or feeling that is new to me.

Today I am feeling ready to put on my traveling shoes. There is a whole world out there to observe.

Open,

Me

How would you describe yourself in social settings?

What do you think about being an observer?

Oh, the Roles We Play on the Stage of Our Life

April 11, 2024

Dear Betty,

First stop on the journey has me thinking about the many roles we play during our lifetime. I have been a wife, mother, grandmother, friend, great grandmother, facilitator, entrepreneur, artist, and story-teller. "Widow" is my most recent title. What exactly does it mean? No, I know what it means, the question might be what does a widow do? What are the expectations of a widow? Should the title widow define who I am now? All of the other titles or roles that I have been or played in my life came with some sort of job description. There were cultural and relationship guidelines about who I was and how I should live my life. They prescribed my behaviors with my husband, my children, and all of the others along the way.

I wonder how I will feel the first time I have to fill out some form or other and "x" the box that says widow. It will signify someone I was and am not anymore. It says with that one little word that something has changed. A lot of things have changed. If I was proud to be his wife, then I am feeling proud to be his widow. I just wish it might not have happened in my eightieth year. Several years from now would have been appreciated.

Widowed,

Me

What are the roles that you have played with joy?

How do you feel about your life roles today?

Transitions

April 12, 2024

Dear Betty,

When reflecting on the theme of this missive, I came to the realization that life is simply a series of transitions. The Latin word "transire," means to go across and often refers to the process, not the end result. Transitioning is the process of change; the act of moving from one set of characteristics or circumstances to another. It might be instantaneous or a series of steps or phases. Transition to life as an elder can occur gradually or abruptly. Elders can change their character if they see that the present way they conduct themselves holds them back or may cause them loss or harm. They may be motivated to a new way of thinking. The bottom line is, despite the significance of our character traits, we can overcome them as required by personal or cultural demands.

What are character traits? Well, they're the parts of a person's behavior and attitude that makes up their personality. Everyone has character traits, both good and bad. Character traits are the way in which we are perceived. We may use adjectives like patient, faithful, or jealous, friendly, kind, courageous, adventurous, stubborn, or cranky. Events in a person's life and influence from others can cause a person to change his or her attitudes and character traits. However, there are still others who will never change.

Transition to eldering is a process, not a series of discrete events. This transition may be achieved in many different ways and time frames. Transitional changes can be difficult. Fear is a reason for the resistance to change. Fear of the loss of control, of losing our independence, fear that life won't be the same, and even a fear of the unknown. It might be helpful to know there are ways to better manage the transitions, even the difficult ones, by addressing these fears. We may need to make decisions about where to live, handling money, friends, relationships, safety, being able to be in charge of our lives, our rights and responsibilities, living independently, living a healthy lifestyle, and having fun. Sharing our feelings of fear, anxiety, doubt and also our feelings of adventure in facing a new challenge can be helpful. Seeking out another elder with attitude can be a bonus.

I found myself focusing on the part of the definition that says, "elders can change their character". So, in closing I will share just one of my transitional goals. I could say that I see myself as a person quick to offer an opinion. But now I am trying to transition into one who stops short of putting her foot into her mouth and one who is a bit more thoughtful before offering any opinion at all. Sometimes the best words are no words at all. As an elder, I find that choosing my wisdoms carefully makes sharing them most meaningful or as a friend of mine would say, "Golden."

Always changing,

Me

How do you feel about being in a state of transition?

What would you like to see yourself transition to?

Angst

April 14, 2024

Dear Betty,

As I often do, I began my search into my new identity. It turns out that just when I found articles about the stages of grief, there were some definitions that I could live with, and others I could not. They just didn't fit me. This brought me around to one of the things that gives me angst these days.

I am retired and widowed. Now in my eightieth year I have met several other women who share these titles with me. The difference I find in our outlook or how we are proceeding on our life path is this: some of us are following a pattern. It seems that there are certain norms at this life stage just as there are in all of life's stages.

Here is what gives me angst, Betty. I see that I once again do not fit the mold. Other retired and/or widowed women seem to follow the stereotype of what all retired/widowed women do. I want to be clear; I am not saying that following the norm is all bad, it is just not for me. It bothers me when following the norm keeps us from becoming all that we can be or doing the things that we can do now that were not available to us before we retired or widowed. If you need safety in doing what they all do, then do that. But, just for a minute, wonder what else there is.

I came across an article by Sheryl Gehrke in which she tries to define what widowhood is. I will admit that some of her descriptions do fit where I have been, others not so much. Since I am trying to be authentic about my eightieth year, I cannot deny that becoming a widow is part of it and so it is one piece of the puzzle of my life story. "Widowhood is living in a constant state of missing the most intimate relationship. No hand to hold." (I especially miss the holding of hands.)

"Widowhood is being alone in a crowd of people. Feeling sad, even while you're happy. It is looking back, while moving forward. It is hungry, but nothing sounds good." (This is how I have become an observer.) "Widowhood is much more than simply missing their presence. It is becoming a new person, or not. It is fighting every emotion and trying to function in life at the same time." (I am not feeling or thinking of myself as a new person. I am the same person who has worked hard at becoming all that I am and still finding that being a widow is teaching me even more about myself. (This is the part that I will call a graced moment for lack of a better descriptor.)

Being widow,

Me

How do you feel about being an orphan or a widow?

What might help you adjust to a new identity?

Great-Grandparenting

April 17, 2024

Dear Betty,

There was a time when I wondered if I would live to see my grandchildren grow to adulthood. Then I wondered what they would do with their lives or who they would become. What kind of people would they become?

Today I went to my great-granddaughter's preschool for an event called "Donuts with Grownups". I thought that I would learn all about what she was learning and see how she would interact with the other children. Instead, I learned that it was all about watching the children play or trying to play with them in their small child's world. I was definitely feeling out of place. Not just old necessarily, just not in tune with what I thought the event would be and what it was. I am happy that I had the opportunity to spend some time with Caroline.

I still experience all of the wondering questions but now they are about my great-grandchildren. Just like the wondering I did about the grandchildren I am simply hoping for them a good life, and one that they choose wisely. I just want them to be happy. At least some of the time, because that is what life gives us: some of this and some of that. It is how we learn and how we become us.

I guess today saw me still in the observer role. Maybe I will always be that in my eightieth year and beyond. I did have a great lunch with my friend Lis, not as an observer but rather a mutual friend. It was so good!

Different strokes,

Me

How do you see yourself in the observer role?

What would you name the stage you are in now?

Job Descriptions

April 16, 2024

Dear Betty

Today, while searching for a definition for being a widow, what I found was several versions of job descriptions. I am not looking for what I should or shouldn't do but rather who I am in my person. This led me to asking what characteristics apply to widows.

Of course, I had to start with the question, what are character traits? The answer I found had me saying, "Now we are getting somewhere." According to Jenifer Herrity, a career coach at Indeed: "Character traits are part of your behaviors, beliefs and personality that help others understand who you are personally and professionally." Obviously, I am not looking for advice about my professional life, that ship has sailed long ago. Rather, I focused on the part about behaviors, beliefs, and personality.

She also says, "There are many character traits that you can develop, such as honesty, flexibility, and curiosity." I hope that I already have these in my possession. But this information led me to asking, "At eighty are my character traits fully formed, or do I have more learning to do?"

What might the character traits be for a widow? Are they any different or have they changed from my earlier years? Well Betty, I think that I am going to do some exploring on this journey to take a look at the traits that I have in my bag and to see if there are more that I can strive for not only as a widow but as a woman in her eightieth year.

Learning,

Me

What are your most valued character traits?

How do you practice them?

Calm and Content

April 17, 2024

Dear Betty,

Met with the Kindreds yesterday and came away asking myself, "Can you be calm and content?" That's the point, no? However, as I continue my stroll down this path I wondered if one can be calm and not content?"

I seem to find myself, if I am being honest with myself, mostly calm these days. Content? I am not so sure about that. Some days I feel antsy, thinking that I should be doing this or that. Finding it hard to settle, but not feeling anxious or worried, just not content. What is causing this feeling of discontent? I am happy with where I am in my life cycle. I love my home and my beautiful surroundings; I enjoy my dog and days with not a thing on my calendar. So, what's the problem? I think that I should be calm and content at the same time. Most times I am calm and content. When I am not content, I think it is when I let myself fall into the crack of wondering if I am needed. At eighty am I still needed? If I look back at the list of characteristics of a widow, and if I follow the belief that I have some of them then I do have purpose and I am needed. See what I did there? I talked myself right out of the crack.

Now I am feeling both calm and content.

That's it Betty,

Me

How would you describe the times when you are feeling calm? Content?

What do you think about the idea of contentment having something to do with being needed?

Becoming Elder

April 22, 2024

Dear Betty,

The more I think about my life at eighty, the more I am becoming aware that writing to you about it is not so different from writing to you about my grief journey. It is similar in that it makes me focus on the issue at hand. I am wondering if what I am doing in these letters is different in that I am thinking more about my identity, not in the same way that I talked about it earlier. I do not want to keep focusing on being a widow because whether one is a widow or not, we still have to come to grips with being old. On being an elder in our families, with our friends, and in our community.

After all of these years of talking about the aging journey, on becoming an elder, on celebrating this time of life I come around to knowing that I don't have a clue. Now when I try to focus on what I am feeling today I find myself thinking more and feeling less. Perhaps this is where my collection of words comes into play. I started out by saying that I felt like or wanted to act like an observer. I think it is another role to play or a behavior. I suppose the next step logically would be to identify how being an observer makes me feel.

The conclusion after all of this is that if I want to be a healthy and whole elder, I will consider both who I am and what I feel.

Today I feel like *Ah! Ha!*

And then...

Me

What does it mean to you to consider both who you are and what you feel?

How does identifying yourself as an observer work for you?

Transferring

April 23, 2024

Dear Betty,

It's quiet here today and I am sitting and listening to the printer coughing away as it spits out some 100 or more pages of Letters to Betty. I have decided that it is time to give my daughters a copy of our correspondence. Watching the pages come out of the printer gives me pause to think of all of the words I have written. I wonder if they will read them. And, if they do, will they be happy that I wrote them? When do I stop wondering about what my family or others think about who I am and what I do? It did seem to me that seeing the black ink on the white paper of so many pages made me feel like I accomplished something. It also makes me wonder why it was, it seems, that writing about grief was in some ways easier than writing about my eightieth year? Maybe all will come clear as we go on.

I do remember that some days on the grief journey I did feel just as blank as I do today. Both of these undertakings seem to be more similar than different. I guess that there is grief in aging and there was acceptance and awareness in the journey through grief. Maybe I am just transferring one focus to another.

So, for today I will return to ordinary things on an ordinary day.

Tomorrow,

Me

P.S. Dandelions in the yard make me happy!

How will a blank slate give rise to making space for creativity or peace in the silence?

What does a blank slate look like for you?

Is Any Age a New Age?

April 24, 2024

Dear Betty,

This morning I heard that eighty is the new seventy. Maybe I should have paid more attention to my years at seventy. Perhaps then I would know what eighty was all about. I doubt it, Betty.

Yesterday one of my grandsons spouted off with way too much attitude. My first notion was to give it right back to him. I had a whole speech rehearsed in my head. I am so happy to report that my wiser, older self took a minute to ask is this really my problem? No, I didn't think so.

Exactly which issues that involve my grandchildren are mine to respond to? Aren't we olders supposed to be teaching them a higher way of behavior rather than being high handed? I decided that this time I would resort to my observer role. Maybe the opportunity will present itself in the future and I will find my way to teachable moments that are kind but wise. Or, maybe I will be still, I doubt it!

Being,

Me

Do you find it difficult to discern whose problem it is? How do you respond to someone else's problem?

What issues that belong to someone else do I have to respond to and how?

Out with the Youngers

April 26, 2024

Dear Betty,

Last night I went out with Christy, my middle daughter, and Roger, her husband, to begin our tour of Wisconsin taverns. We went to River Mike's. It is definitely a tavern. Lots of locals sitting at the bar and just a few tables. The food was really good and having a beer with Roger is always fun.

I am finding writing about being eighty is much more challenging than writing about my grief. So much of what I am feeling is similar to what I have been feeling during my grief journey that by the way is far from over. Much of the time I am alone on this island of not yesterday but not yet tomorrow either.

When we studied nostalgia, I was right there believing that it is not good to stay nostalgic about the past. Today I think that a little trip back to what has been is not so bad. In fact, the other day I was on a memory trip and it felt like I was watching a slide show of events. Some of them were happy ones, and others not so much. Perhaps it is true that those of us blessed enough to be healthy in our eighties can find a balance between the gift of the past and the unknown of the future.

Today I am feeling quite positive, happy almost. Today I feel more like seventy-ish than what the calendar tells me is happening in my eightieth year. In short: time just keeps marching on. I know that I will find the right tune one of these days. What is the theme song for the eighties?

Trusting,

Me

How do you relate to the idea of not yesterday but not yet tomorrow?

What do you think about taking a memory trip once in a while?

A Shared Journey

April 27, 2024

Dear Betty,

What can I tell you today about my travels through time in my eightieth year? So far it seems to me that now three months into this journey I have come to believe that one thing is for sure: grief and aging at eighty share the road ahead.

My dear friend is suffering and I am sure is close to death. I had been holding so much hope for her but after our phone call last night it became clear to me that soon I will be grieving yet again. When I hung up the phone I was once again overwhelmed by sadness.

Betty, there *is* so much loss at this stage of life. Loss of things that I have known. Like hearing her voice telling me who I am and what I should do. Who will tell me these things when she is gone? One of the sadnesses I recognized was her inability to stay on the phone for any kind of lengthy conversation. How I wish I could be with her.

Once again, I cried. Accepting the truth of what is never gets easier and I suspect it will be another of those companions that we olders live with but wish we didn't have to experience. Betty, I own that I am a selfish person, I don't want to think of her suffering, it is not how I want to remember our time together.

Having said that, I am so sad that she is suffering but so enriched by her faith and steadfastness. I love her.

Sad,

Me

What can you do to help you accept the "what is" of life?

How do you envision your own journey into the sixties, seventies, eighties and beyond?

Weddings With the Olders is Fun

April 28, 2024

Dear Betty,

Feeling grateful today. Last evening my older daughter Caryn and I went to a family wedding. I was able to visit with my first cousins. They are all in their eighties and so it was very interesting to listen to their conversations.

They are all fun and funny. They are full of stories about how all of us grew up. The conversation was typical of how conversations take form in our eighties. It went from who had the most recent surgery, to who was not present because they are too ill to attend. Then suddenly the conversation shifted to stories from our collective past to what they thought of this modern wedding and who would be rolling over in their graves. They engaged in the wedding, celebrating in just the way that they know how, dancing and enjoying one another's company. They are great role models for those of us entering this stage of our eldering journey. Best of all they talk about those who are no longer with us with love and respect and not at all with melancholy, but as though they were sitting right there enjoying the party with us.

I am so grateful that they have been a part of my life and I regret that we just don't see one another often enough. Last night was one that I am so glad I was able to share with my daughter. It is one for the ages and one that I am happy to document today. I am also grateful for my health and my somewhat stable mental acuity.

We left with hugs and promises to try to get together again soon. I hope that we can.

Glad,

Me

How do you feel about celebrating with your older relatives or friends?

What kind of gatherings make you happy?

Could Do Without the Ride

April 29, 2024

Dear Betty,

I wonder if this my eightieth year will always feel like a roller coaster. Ups and downs, carried away by moments of excitement and happiness and then moments of uncertainty or sadness. Betty, I felt so filled with belonging and happiness while being with my senior cousins. I am the second youngest and they like to remind me of this often. Each of them told stories about our growing up together, their eyes alive with the remembering.

Yesterday, I felt the knowing pain of an older once again. Questions present themselves like unwanted guests. Will I see them again? Will there be another opportunity for this precious few to laugh and tell stories and pick on one another again? I do not recall having these questions as we lived through the forties, fifties, sixties, and on to now our eighties.

Life was happening for all of us. We were raising families or working at careers or taking care of the then elders. We didn't see one another any more often but it didn't seem to cause any alarm because of course we had all of the time in the world. It seems, Betty, that a reoccurring theme for me now in my eightieth year is questioning. I must say however, that I find myself appreciating those few senior cousins more and more. I love who they are and what they, without even knowing it, are teaching me about who I might be moving forward in this extraordinary year. They are eccentric and they own their authentic selves and they have earned the right many times over. Now I find that it makes me happy, just thinking about them.

As an older,

Me

What are the unwanted guests in your life now?

Does the metaphor of a roller coaster hold true for you, how?

Music Can Soothe the Soul

April 30, 2024

Dear Betty,

This morning I turned on the T.V. to find the music channel. I found one that was playing symphonies and concertos. I was immediately mesmerized. Sitting there on the tuffet, I felt completely present to what was happening there, right in my living room. The music was a little soulful, soft, and repetitive. Then they changed to a rousing tune and I wish I could remember its name.

Last evening, I found myself thinking about the difference between being resigned and accepting. I guess I was trying to stay focused on this assignment about reflecting on my eightieth year. The music brought me to, I believe, one of the pivotal moments in my life. My parents moved us from the city to a small rural community. I would have been attending a large parochial school in the fall but I found myself instead in a small public school and very much an outsider. What has this to do with music, resignation, or acceptance? All of these years later, I can say that I would have viewed music differently had I had the opportunity to join an orchestra. I instead played the accordion in my dad's dance hall. I believe that in that year and many that followed, I accepted my life as being just what it should be knowing full well that it would change at some time in the future. I don't believe that I was ever just resigned.

Now at eighty, things like listening to the music brought me to wondering how my life might have been different. I am very sure that it would have been but I don't think that it is helpful to my process now to stay with this question. I think that it is more productive to decide if I am now accepting my days ahead or am I resigned to them.

I am willing to accept the choices that were made for me or that I made for myself as meaningful. I have had a good, good life. I am also willing to say that I am somewhat resigned to what is to come. What other choice is there?

Present,

Me

What is the difference between resigning and accepting in your mind?

What soothes your soul these days?

May

Excuses

May 5, 2024

Dear Betty,

It has been a couple of days since I have written. I am sorry. It has been a busy time full of emotional stuff and ordinary stuff. Making my way to your letter just didn't happen. I could make all kinds of excuses but instead I will just say that I will be taking the time this week to process all of it with you.

Maybe then writing to you will help me gain some perspective. I have been thinking a lot about perspective. Still thinking about what it means to be resigned and for heaven's sake not at all wanting to be reticent.

Till later,

Me

How would you talk about the times in your life when you were resigned or reticent?

When do you feel that you need to be excused? What do you do then?

Tidal Waves

May 6, 2024

Dear Betty,

It is Monday. Last Thursday I went to the laboratory for a blood draw because I was to see the doctor today. As I was driving to the hospital, I was feeling light, confident, and proud of myself. I was driving myself, knowing exactly where I had to go and what I needed to do. All was well. When I was leaving the lab however, I found myself walking down the hospital halls just like I had done so many times before, only this time it was me leaving the lab and not me waiting outside in the car for Don. The memories came rushing in like a tidal wave of the kind of sadness that I had not felt in some time. It was not the everyday kind of sad that will be with me for all of the rest of my days. No, it was the kind of sadness from my early days of grief. Tears, loneliness, and the reality of my life now and I surmise the rest of my eightieth year and beyond. It was an all-day event.

My morning reflection today informs me that embarking on my eightieth year with all of its unknowing is not so very different from the unknowing around the issue of my grief journey. Like the ring I had made from Don's class ring, they are entwined, braided together, so like the way I perceive my body, soul, and spirit. As he would often say, "It is what it is." So again, I practice resignation.

Good day,

Me

Have you ever felt like your emotions were surfacing for you like a tidal wave?

What do you think about the phrase "It is what it is"?

Perspective

May 7, 2024

Dear Betty,

"Your perspective is the way you see something. Perspective has a Latin root meaning 'look through' or 'perceive,' and all the meanings of perspective have something to do with looking, a way of thinking about and understanding something." Vocabulary .com

While thinking about how I see myself at eighty, I wondered how my perspective played a role in how I see myself, what I think about aging and how it all makes me feel. Perhaps I thought, I need to identify who my role models might be or who they might have been up to this point.

Other things to consider are the many questions that keep arriving at the door of my reverie or on my tablet. Here is one from just the other day, it is from a book I am reading called *The Grace of Aging* by Katleen Cowling Singh: "New questions emerge, often clamoring for attention. Who am I beyond the functions I've served? Who am I when the habits of a lifetime are stripped away? Who am I beyond the persona I've presented to the world and to myself? Who am I, bare?"

I will delve into them, Betty, but not today.

Procrastinating,

Me

How do you feel about the new questions that appear in your life journey?

What does perspective mean to you?

Has your perspective changed recently? How?

A Soft Chair

May 8, 2024

Dear Betty,

Today I was invited out to lunch with my grandson Jake and my daughter Caryn. It was lovely to be asked. We went to a café in a little town near here that is known for its family style atmosphere and its all–day breakfast. Caryn's favorite.

After lunch we visited Nik, my grandson. We had really bad storms last night and a large tree fell onto his house. It was the first time I had been to his home since Don and I visited shortly after he moved into it. Both of those grandsons always make me feel welcome and special. I listened to the conversation and surveyed the damage caused by the unruly tree. I thought to myself, *this is just the kind of thing that Don was good at.* He would have known just what to say and what to tell Nik about how to take care of the situation.

I, on the other hand, found myself thinking or rather reminding myself that I was in observer training. You know what Betty, I felt pretty comfortable just being there with the young people listening and paying attention to the difference in how their conversations evolve.

So, no answering pending questions today. Just grateful for the opportunity to spend some time with the youngsters. One observation, I am pleasantly tired now and really ready to be welcomed into my soft chair for a while before the afternoon wanes away.

Happy,

Me

Do you have a soft chair, a space in which you feel comforted?

What do you think about listening to what is around you and not having to respond?

Aunties

May 10, 2024

Dear Betty,

I have been thinking a lot about the question: who are the models for me at this stage of life? I will attempt to begin to answer that question for you today.

The matriarch of my mother's family was my auntie, Bobbie. Her name was really Barbara. It seems that it was a thing for our family to name their children after either their mother or father or close other relatives. Hence there are a lot of Barbaras in the family. I was named Mary Margaret after two aunts and a grandmother.

Auntie Bobbie has certainly been an important presence in my life. She was self-less, loving, kind, and creative. When her mother died and her father committed suicide, she married at the age of 13 to take care of her siblings. She was never able to finish her schooling but she taught, I think, the most important things in life. One of my most recurring memories of Auntie Bobbie is seeing her in her kitchen wearing a cobbler apron that she made out of colorful cotton. She made them and sold them to help provide for husband and their five children. Her door was always open and there was always time for coffee and a *schneck*. It is the memory of her voice however that makes me smile each time I remember her greeting, "Honey, come."

Everyone was honey to her and each of us felt loved always.

If I have only loved half as much as Auntie Bobbie did then in the end I can say, I too was a loving person. She never stopped being herself. She is my model of love, persistence, and generosity.

Tomorrow, Auntie Theresa,

Me

Can you name the women in your life who have influenced your view of aging?

What is the history of your name? Do you have a namesake?

Mother's Day

May 12, 2024

Dear Betty,

Before I continue telling you about the women I want to see as my role models, I feel that I need to tell you how I woke up this morning. It may in some way relate to a role model. We'll see.

I got out of bed feeling rather stiff but after sitting in my very soft and comfortable chair with my morning coffee I remembered something about my mom. She liked to cut things out of the newspaper. Recipes, poems, and once in a while, something that tickled her fancy. She once cut out a piece that talked about arthritis, or, as they called in the article, "Arthur I Tis". It was about waking up and realizing that Arthur had visited. It went on with a litany of all of the things that he affected. Well, I thought mom was right, this morning I was visited by Arthur as well. After the time of sitting and drinking my coffee I felt considerably better and went on with my day.

This experience also brought me to a deeper appreciation of the pain that Don, my mom and others suffer, some to a much greater degree than I. It also made me feel so very grateful for the good health that I am able to enjoy in this my eightieth year.

It is Mother's Day and so appropriate that I would remember this story about my mom. I have also been invited to lunch with a daughter, grandchildren, and great-grandchildren. So, Betty, another role model will wait until tomorrow.

Today is the day,

Me

What are you grateful for today in regards to your health?

How does this story relate to you and empathy?

Not So Crazy

May 13, 2024

Dear Betty,

Aunt Teresa or Aunt Tree was certainly an influence in my life. To most of the family she was crazy. I thought she was interesting and eccentric and I loved her for it. She wore colorful house dresses and an apron that went over her head, probably made by her sister auntie Bobbie. She was not the best of cooks but she was very creative in trying new things in the kitchen. She loved to tell stories. Aunt Tree had a gold lamé party dress that she wore for all of the family weddings and sometimes even for other family parties. She was fun and I loved her. It was only in her older years that she was finally diagnosed as being bipolar. By this time, she lived in a nursing home and was receiving treatment. I don't recall her ever saying a cross word, even when others were not kind to her, and many were.

One time at a gathering of a group of women I belonged to, the question was asked, how do you see yourself as you age? Or, who do you want to be? My answer was, "I want to be authentic, eccentric, and wise." I think Aunt Tree was all of them. If only others would have looked beyond her quirks and fancies, they would have seen them as well.

I wonder if I will ever reach the level of authenticity, eccentricity, or wisdom that she modeled for me? I am committed to trying, just not sure I have the courage or hutzpah. At eighty, it may well be worth the effort.

Love to Aunt Tree,

Me

What do you think about the story of Aunt Tree?

Have you ever felt misunderstood like you might be the crazy one?

Pocketbooks

May 13, 2024

Dear Betty,

Do you know what a pocketbook is? Well, my auntie Margaret was never without hers. Today we call them bags or purses. Auntie Margaret was a tall willowy woman with an amazing quick wit and a one-of-a-kind sense of humor. She was a house wife who, just like Aunt Tree, wore cotton house dresses and was never without her apron. Unlike Aunt Tree, she was a really good cook. No one would say that her meals were fancy but they were for sure down home tasty comfort food. One of her specialties was bread dumplings. Ah, fond memories.

As a role model I would choose her for her hospitality and her rock-solid presence to her family and to me. You see Betty, I went to school just down the street from her house. Once a week my cousins and I would walk to her house for lunch. Grilled cheese or pan-fried mac and cheese were well worth the walk. Auntie Margaret is one of my namesakes. My cousins, who are now in their eighties, each have her sense of fun, humor, and quick wit. They are a joy to be with as was their mother. A role model for sure.

Smiling,

Me

Did you know what a pocketbook was?

Do you have any stories like this one about Auntie Margaret?

What is your favorite story about someone who might be a role model for you?

Sister Aunties

May 13, 2024

Dear Betty,

Sister to Auntie Margaret is my Auntie Mary. I was named for both of them and a few others as well. Auntie Mary was a professional woman. She married Uncle Charlie and never had children. They were like second parents to Auntie Margaret's kids though.

Auntie Mary rode the bus to work every day. She was very stylish. The most stylish of all of my aunties. She was the only one who was brave enough to wear slacks. They may have been called trousers back then. I knew her to be soft spoken and always dressed in the latest styles, only the tasteful ones of course. She was for sure someone that I admired, even then when I was just in my early teens. She and Uncle Charlie were very generous. It was always a treat to visit their house at Christmas time. Auntie Mary always had a white flocked tree with blue shiny ornaments on it. Gifts and chocolates were part of the visit and there was always a lot of conversation among the adults. There was laughter, good food, and warm happy feelings.

Auntie Mary was a progressive woman before anyone would think of naming her that. What I want to emulate about her now was her way of being, just who she was but she did it with so much grace. She was unassuming. I don't think that she ever thought that she was better than others. She was just happy being Charlie's wife, and a working woman who was kind, gracious, and generous.

Well-named,

Me

Is there a woman in your history who you admired and still admire today?

What is it that you admire in her?

How do you feel about breaking away from social norms, like wearing slacks when others weren't?

Stalwarts

May 16, 2024

Dear Betty,

I find it so very interesting that in searching for my role models I found my way to my aunties. Of course, there have been many women who have crossed my path. Some of them I could count as role models but it comes to me that they were instead like learning companions. Each one of them taught me something about myself or the world around me. Some have had more impact than others and they are still challenging me to be my better self.

What drew me to my aunties was their stalwartness. They wouldn't have spent time thinking about a blueprint for their eightieth year. No, they just continued to go about their ordinary tasks as they looked at each day as being just what it was supposed to be. They had a simple and practical faith that led them to face the loss of years with grace. Betty, I don't think that I can be half as graceful or as settled in myself as they seemed to be. One can only hope.

What I know about being eighty so far is that grief remains a ghost of the past and a harbinger of the future. Still, grief gives us the gift of loving, of remembering, of feeling things, of understanding that would not be unwrapped without it. Is it pleasant? Of course not. But when I embrace it, I find myself owning parts of myself that I didn't even know were there.

Was I looking for a blueprint for my eighties? I guess I was and that is what brought me to looking for role models. Now I know that it will only be written after the fact. At sixty, one thinks about hurrying to complete unfinished business. At seventy, one tries to figure out what happened to all of the other years and to wonder if a plan needs to be made. Now, at eighty I can choose to go about just the ordinary days and things of my life or I can choose to continue writing to you because you help me find my way. Writing to you inspires me to think and feel my way through eighty.

While thinking about blueprints or role models or someone who might share with me a magic bullet of age, I came across many books about aging. As I discovered when I was looking for answers for grief, they all say basically the same thing and none of them address my way of processing. So, Betty, you are stuck with me.

Be you,

Me

How do you see yourself as being stalwart?

What qualities do you think you most admire in women you have met along the way of your life?

What helps you to continue learning and growing in these older years?

To Plan or Not

May 17, 2024

Dear Betty,

What is it that makes me want to have a plan for my life this year? I know Betty, it is easier to check off the list of what I should be doing and who I should be. Today I realize that I need to let go of wanting someone else's thoughts on the subject. I need to forget about what should be and stay in the present of what is now.

Thus said, today I am feeling deeply sad. My best friend is dying and there is not one bloody thing that I can do about it. I am tired of grief and loss but today I am trying to accept that it is what life is like at eighty. In a book that my friend Linda Piotrowski wrote she described those she has lost or rather the memory of those that she has lost as the ghosts in her life. Now I am beginning to understand what she meant. I see the transparent forms and actions of those that I have lost and, in some ways, it gives me solace to recognize my own ghosts. They are a different kind of memory than the ones conjured up in my mind or when looking at pictures. They just appear sitting at the kitchen table, or at the kitchen sink, sitting on the porch, or working in the garden. Although my friend still lives, she is on the other side of the country. She already comes to me as one of my friendly ghosts. I see us walking to the coffee shop, drinking a glass of wine on a warm summer day, and laughing.

You make me smile Betty, even on sad days like this. I wonder what tomorrow will bring. Still, it was good to spend some time with the aunties and I hope that I will do them proud in each of my days.

Eighty and counting,

Me

What do you think it means to stay in the present?

How do you feel about Linda's description of the ghosts in her life?

Was it helpful for you to think about women in your past who have impacted you?

Role Models

May 20, 2024

Dear Betty,

I am still thinking about role models. Do you think that I would ever be a role model? If I think about this, I wonder what characteristics I might aspire to exhibit at this stage of a life full of so much of everything. What was I like or what did I do during the growing stages of marriage and parenting? How did I react to the really good stuff and the not-so-great stuff? Is it worth it to go back through the pages of my story to learn the answers to these questions? Maybe it would only make me feel remorseful sinking into the fear of regret. Shoulda, woulda, coulda.

On the other hand, maybe I would learn that I had and maybe still have the characteristics that got me through, made me happy, created in me a loving soul. Was it the characteristics? Or was I just too naïve in my youth to understand or to name qualities in myself? I will say that faith and intuition have been consistent companions for me. Women of my age were not really encouraged to think about these things. Like my stoic mother and my matter-of-fact aunties, I think that we just faced each day with whatever resources we had gleaned. I do think that unfortunately there are too many women who were not given the chance to become emotionally intelligent, strong women. Maybe they were not as blessed as me with aunties or other role models to help them on their way. I have encountered many women who have been deprived of the joy of having role models.

Eighty, learning and growing,

Me

How have you experienced faith and intuition in your life?

Do you find it interesting to think about role models at this stage of life and how you have grown because of them?

Herding Sheep

May 21, 2024

Dear Betty,

Today I started out doing ordinary things. I anticipated having a rather quiet day catching up on phone calls and other odds and ends. After running my errands, I got home and took my dog York out to play. Just as I was settling down to think about the rest of my day and my letter to you, the phone rang and it sent me out the door. The sheep were out on the road and something had to be done until Jake, my grandson who is a farmer, could arrive to secure the little trouble makers in the pasture where they belong. Fortunately, I am getting really good at herding with Mini, my Kubota runabout.

A really nice guy driving by stopped his truck, put on his hazard lights and did not hesitate helping me shoo them off of the road. Someone must have called the Sheriff because soon there were two squad cars with flashing lights coming our way. They all helped us, Jake arrived, and soon all was well again.

Hours later I am sitting here wondering if there is a lesson or another description of who I might be or what I might do at eighty. Do I respond to the unexpected without having to ponder all of the consequences? Do I use the resources that I have at hand? How am I appreciating help gracefully? I suspect that these are questions I may be asking myself more than just this once as this year continues. For today, I feel pretty proud of myself and once again so grateful for Mini.

A question for tomorrow, Betty: can one be calm but not content?

Naughty sheep are still kinda cute,

Me

How do you respond to the unexpected?

How willing are you to ask for help?

What surprises you when you find yourself in unexpected circumstances?

Sanctuary

May 22, 2024

Dear Betty,

There is a lovely small Episcopal Church here in my town. I went to church there last Sunday. It was a pleasant experience. First of all, the church itself is warm and welcoming. Old wooden beams look down on old and comfortable pews. The folks were also warm and welcoming. Best of all, I knew the words to the prayers that we were asked to pray together. It has been some time since I visited a church on a Sunday morning. On any morning actually. It has been a longing that I have noticed recently in myself. I do like the feeling of a small community and since I was raised in a faith-filled family who went to church every Sunday, I do appreciate the ritual of the service. I enjoyed singing Gregorian Chant and volunteered to do that often in the church of my youth. As I sat in the smooth, solid pew with the sun highlighting the stained glass windows, I felt calm.

I found a description in the Miriam-Webster Dictionary of what it means to be content; being content is more about a general sense of well-being and peace with one's life. Although I did feel calm waiting sitting in that pew on Sunday, I cannot say that I was content. Then I began to wonder what the difference might be between being content and being satisfied.

I have concluded that for me being satisfied is more about my everyday walking through this time of my life. Can I say that I am content each day, that I have come to some understanding about what this year of eighty might be? Truthfully, I will only say that I am for the most part calm. Content, not so much. Still too many things to understand, too many questions to find the answers for. If I accomplish even some awareness and acceptance perhaps then I will be calm and content at the same time. Or at least with some aspects of my glorious old life.

I found this prose recently and thought it worth sharing: "To live content with small means, to seek elegance rather than luxury, and refinement rather than fashion, to be worthy, not respectable, and wealthy, not rich, think quietly, talk gently, act frankly, to listen to stars and birds, to babes and sages, with open heart, to bear all cheerfully, to all bravely await occasions, hurry never, in a word, to let the spiritual unbidden and unconscious grow up through the common. This is to be my symphony." – William Henry Channing

Trying calmness,

Me

Where do you find sanctuary?

How do you find times of calmness?

When do you feel content?

Contradictions

May 23, 2024

Dear Betty,

I continue to be proud of myself. Things that I thought I could not do by myself have lost their hold on me. Yesterday I went to the dermatologist by myself. I see her at the hospital and that alone is a bit daunting, mostly because it reminds me of all of the times I was with Don at doctor's offices and at the hospital. It felt good to realize that I could be independent in this way. I suppose it has to do with not wanting to be a bother to someone. I do not want to think of myself as being needy either, or if I am honest, maybe I hope that someone will see my need and they would offer. This is a contradiction. "Which is it?" I say to myself.

My right knee is acting up and so it makes me think again about the aging body that we have no control over. I realize that I may well be on the way to being pushed around in a wheelchair or at the very least using a "stick". Is this it Betty, is this what eighty is all about? I think that I will try to focus on the positives. I am really very healthy for my age and I much prefer thinking about more ethereal things.

Wondering,

Me

How hard is it for you to ask for help, see yourself as needy?

What are the contradictions that you are facing now?

Choosing Our Memories

May 24, 2024

Dear Betty,

My dearest friend Dre is terminally ill and living in Florence, Oregon. I cannot go to her but we talk often. I am not so sure that I want to see her physically. I want to look at the picture of the two of us when we were both much younger. That is the memory that I want to keep in my heart. We laughed and told each other what our friendship has meant to each of us over the years. She has the sexiest voice with just a tinge of California accent. She talks about being terminal with such hope and confidence in how she wants to approach this last part of her life journey. She for sure is a role model. Talking to her made me start to think about how I am approaching this year. Is it with hope or expectation?

Betty, don't you think that we bring expectation to each part, each stage of our life journey? I haven't really been thinking about what my expectations are now. I know that I can expect more news of grief, friends, and family either declining or dying. I expect that my own health will begin to take new twists and turns. I expect that my children and grandchildren will start to see me differently. I expect that I will not be as interested in some things but more interested in things that I haven't thought about before.

Ah, but even though I find it hard to think about my expectations I find that somewhere in my days now there is hope. I hope that I can remain as independent as I am now at eighty for some time to come. I hope that I can continue to have meaningful relationships. I hope that I will continue to grow mentally and spiritually. I hope that I will always remember Don lovingly, kindly, humanly, and with a smile on my face.

OK, so thinking about expectations and hope can easily lead me to gratitude. I have plenty of it but for now I will refrain from making the gratitude list. I am sure though that I want to say how grateful I am for you Betty. You are amazing!

Hopeful Expectations,

Me

How do you feel about the idea of choosing memories?

What are your most cherished memories and who are they about?

Planting Will Never be the Same

May 25, 2024

Dear Betty,

It is Memorial Day weekend. This is the weekend that was for 20 years the weekend that the whole family gathered to plant the gardens. It was one of Don's most favorite days. He planned for weeks ahead, bought plants and ordered seeds. He rototilled each of the gardens and for the most part he was ready when the big day arrived. He loved going from garden to garden to tease the planters and to make sure that they were planting the correct things in each garden.

This Memorial Day weekend only one garden will get planted. The raised bed gardens that the grandsons built last year will be filled and when all is finished, we will gather to spread Don's ashes. I thought that I was well prepared for this day, in fact I am not well prepared. I wish we would have done it sooner but still Betty, it seems fitting that this memorial to him should happen on one of the days and with those he loved the most.

Sometimes it is hard to fulfill promises made to someone you love. We talked about what would happen when this day came. You can be as prepared as you think you are but, in the end, love is love and grief is grief, and sadness remains. At eighty, it is no surprise to me, this end time. So here we are Betty, I will take care of this wish of his and I will continue to put one foot in front of the other with purpose and gratitude for each of my ordinary days but hoping that there will be many extraordinary times as well.

Courage, please bless me today,

Me

What promises about last wishes have you had to fulfill?

How do you share wishes you may have as you age?

Rainy Days

May 26, 2024

Dear Betty,

"Rainy Days and Mondays" is a song that I was reminded of this morning. I have to admit that I do not object to all rainy days or for that matter all Mondays. Today, however, it is not only rainy but dreary as well.

Tomorrow, which is Memorial Day, we will scatter Don's ashes. I am beginning to be aware that I am affected more by the weather these days. Maybe I am just more aware of the makeup of every day now. I notice that on cloudy or rainy days I am more likely to want to stay in and withdraw from the world and maybe even my desire to be present to my aging life issues. On sunny days, I seem to have more energy and I sense a willingness to grab the tiger by the tail and get on with it already.

I am somewhat conflicted about scattering Don's ashes. I know that I have to do it because that is what he wanted. Still, there is some comfort in having his ashes here in the house with me. I will see it done tomorrow and I will allow myself the space today to feel dreary. Maybe a while in my chair with a blanket and a warm cup of chocolate would not go amiss.

Drip, Drip, Drip,

Me

What can you do when you are feeling dreary?

How do you manage your rainy days?

Scattered Ashes

May 28, 2024

Dear Betty,

The family gathered, we scattered the ashes and without words I could tell that each of us was lost to their own grief, letting go, and present, but not present.

It seemed for me an out of body experience. I was surely there in body but it will take some time to describe exactly where I was in spirit and soul. Grief overwhelmed me yet again. I recognize it now and I refuse to let it consume me. I acknowledge it, recognize it, and honor it. I am changed because of it. New exploration to consider, and I will.

Today I am pondering once again my role as widow. I am no longer a wife and with yesterday's ritual completed I no longer have wifely duties to perform. My dear friend was very clear with me the other day when she said that it was time for me to stop being the director of each family event. She accused me of being like an actress who plays a role. Now she said, "You have to be yourself. Let someone else be in charge."

Are there really no more wifely duties? What about continuing to be with our family in the way that we valued? I would feel remorse and somewhat guilty if I stopped being the person that I was with him. Is it my duty to preserve the story that led us to living our lives caring and loving and holding to our truths? I believe that I have done all of the things that he asked me to do. Perhaps since I am no longer a wife, I will relinquish wifely duties. Perhaps I will instead look to the other roles that I still have before me: widow, mother, grandmother, great-grandmother, friend, and teacher.

It all seems too much on this day so I think I will go back once again to the ordinary thing. I will do the laundry and spend the day reflecting on yesterday because I believe that then I will be more inclined to embrace tomorrow.

In the quiet today,

Me

How do you manage the scattered ashes of your life?

What are the roles that you have recognized and moved on from?

Being and Doing

May 29, 2024

Dear Betty,

It occurs to me today that I may have been pursuing this attempt to define my life at eighty without experiencing it. What if I stop thinking about how I should be in this my eightieth year and focus more on *who* I am being. Back to the old saying about being a human being and not a human doing. Actually, I think we have to be both of those things.

If I focus more on going about my every day just as it comes to me will I be writing to you in retrospect? How can I tell you about the learnings of each day before I have experienced it? Perhaps it comes to both being in the moment or rather the day or year and pondering the what and how of it.

I continue to be fascinated by words and their meanings. Today I am wondering about the difference between acknowledging, accepting, and awareness. Acknowledging is knowing that yep, I am eighty, can't change it, try to accept it because it just is. Awareness for me is being present to what is around me. Maybe noticing would be another descriptive word that works for me. Noticing what I am doing, how I am doing it, how do I feel about it. Noticing the others around me, what they are feeling, thinking, or doing?

Denying any age is to deny the grace of the moment. I don't want to be at the end of whatever age I may live to and then face the regret of not having acknowledged the events that have made me who I am at eighty or hopefully beyond.

Ah, awareness,

Me

How do I become an aging person who continues to do what life calls me to do?

What changes invite me into the being of my life, like being authentic in my body, mind, and spirit?

Slow or Fast

May 30, 2024

Dear Betty,

Today I heard someone say, "I am going slow now because for too long I was going fast." I really like this thought. I think I should make a poster of it and put it somewhere I can see it often. Going slow is one of the things that I have been kicking and screaming about these days. The idea of going slow does give one permission to be present and really experience each day fully.

Yesterday I was telling you about the words acknowledging, accepting, and awareness. Today I see that they fit very well with going slow. I don't feel as though I have to worry too much about acknowledging my age, as that is what I have been writing to you about these months. I am accepting that it is what it is. Being aware, however, is the one that seems to come along with going slow.

Is going slow different than slowing down? What do you think Betty? I think that slowing down means that I am still trying to go fast, to be busy, to find things to do, to be involved, and that I have to slow my roll. Going slow, Betty, is for me more about starting at the stop sign and then moving through the intersection of life with intention, cautiously paying attention. Going slow is not an easy goal when everything in our culture keeps telling us to go fast no matter what age we are.

An advertisement on the T.V. This morning said seniors should be about active aging. Doesn't the word active alone imply living fast? If the meaning were to see active aging as participating in one's own aging process, whether that may be fast or slow, accepting the inevitable progress of time, I could go along with it. It was not the intention of the advertisement I am sure. It continued on to promote an event where "elders" could socialize, learn about programs, exercise, volunteer, and travel. All the things that we aging folk are "supposed to be about." For those of us who find joy and peace in all of the "supposed tos", I say hail and good cheer. Betty, for those of us who choose to go slow, I would appreciate just a little more respect for our way of graceful aging.

For the love of slow,

Me

Which do you choose? Fast or slow?

How do you describe graceful aging?

A Little Fantasy

May 31, 2024

Dear Betty,

Once again, I have spent the week in grief. Yes, I know it is never very far away from my door and it always resides to some extent in my heart. Yet when it returns with its full force, I cannot help but feel overwhelmed.

Thankfully it doesn't seem to last as long, the loud clang turns into the softer tones of the wind chimes outside of my back door.

There must be some grace in reality and at the best of my times I fully accept that. Still, I would rather take a moment in my slow going to let my mind float off into the unrealistic. We all need a bit of fantasy in our lives don't you think?

I thought a lot about balance last night. It seems that we always come back to balance but I am beginning to think that I enjoy more of the slow-going than the fast-going of the world's expectations of my aging process. Perhaps I might try to enjoy the fast-going if I try to be present to it and see the value in it.

Slow can be lonely at times and fast exhausting. In my life I will acknowledge them both.

I wonder if I will feel the same way at the end of my eightieth year?

Sorting it out,

Me

Does everything always come back to balance?

Where is the grace in reality?

How will you let a bit of fantasy into your heart?

JUNE

Let's Be Emotional

June 1, 2024

Dear Betty,

I have come to a new understanding of what my sudden outpouring of tears is all about. Grief, I thought, will it never stop? Probably not. I still believe this. Today, however, I was watching a success story on the morning news. The man being interviewed was choking back tears and apologizing for having a moment. The interviewer was very kind and allowed him to take a moment to compose himself.

Here is my conclusion; I too had tears in my eyes just watching and listening to this story. Why is this affecting me? I believe that those of us who strive to be compassionate and even empathic, become more emotional as we age. Don was a good example of this. He was not a guy who sought attention and for the most part kept his feelings to himself. But, as he aged, he could get teary at the smallest things: a greeting card, song lyrics and even comments from the kids. I think that this is what is happening to me. Yes, I am still having grief tears but I do believe that I am more outwardly emotional. I hope that I am becoming a kinder, gentler self, willing to be touched by all manner of things. The stories of others, a lovely birdsong, a kind comment from a friend, overwhelming beauty around me and the coming and going of my grandchildren.

So, Betty, not all of my tears are sad ones. Some are happy and some are grateful. Mostly I am pleased today to recognize a new understanding of myself. I accept my aging emotional self. At the end of the day, all tears are salty.

Emotionally yours,

Me

Why not show our kinder, gentler self?

What makes you feel emotional and are you OK with it?

Acceptance is the Bane of Aging

June 2, 2024

Dear Betty,

Last night I invited Christy, Roger, and Caryn to dinner. It was a pleasant evening and I enjoyed making the simple supper. The best part was after dinner. We sat in the living room and just visited about nothing in particular. It was really nice to have someone to share a meal with at the table and not on T.V. trays in front of the T.V.

Later after all had left, I got a call from Dre. She is progressing through her illness and is accepting these days as best as she can. It makes me so sad that I cannot be with her. I am, however, so remarkably blessed to be able to enjoy our phone conversations. I didn't sleep well. Memories and the reality of what is to come to soon. Acceptance is the bane of aging.

Kicking and screaming,

Me

How can we accept all of the aging losses with grace?

What can we do when we want to kick and scream rather than accept?

Energy and Expectations

June 3, 2024

Dear Betty,

I have been noticing that lately my energy level does not match up with my expectations. If this is true when I am going about my everyday life, then, I think it is a good thing that I didn't begin this year with great expectations. In fact, I don't think that I had any expectations other than the obvious ones of more crags and crevices on my face, my arms getting just a bit looser and more flappable, my appetite waning, my hair thinning even more and bedtime arriving before the 10 o'clock news. I may plan several ordinary things that I hope to accomplish on any given day. I plunge headlong into my list. Later that day, or even the next, I am exhausted. Thus, the realization that I no longer have the energy to meet my expectations. Back to going slow, because going fast is possible, but I think not so smart.

I suppose that even though I have never been one to follow the norm, that I should probably think about expectations. But if I go down that road, will I be disappointed if they don't come to fruition? What are my great expectations? What is the difference between expectations and having hope? Here is what Google says:

"Both describe beliefs about the future. An expectation, however, is a strong belief that things will be or should be a certain way, and an attachment to the outcome. A hope is a desire for an outcome, a wish with some uncertainty about what will actually transpire. We cling to expectations, and hold loosely to hopes."

I am going to opt for hope. If I start creating expectations for myself then I fear that I will once fall into being in control. I have spent too much time trying not to have to control everything, thinking that things have to be a certain way. I like the idea of "let the chips fall where they may," within reason of course. I hope that I can remain healthy and remain independent. I hope for all good for my children and grandchildren, even the grans (my great–grandchildren.) I hope for friendships that endure and family love and I hope that my memories serve me well and finally I hope that I continue this my eightieth year with grace and good humor.

Hoping,

Me

When you feel like you have less energy, what do you believe the reason might be?

How do you deal with the fact that your energy level does not meet up with your expectations of yourself?

Tears

June 5, 2024

Dear Betty,

I am so extremely sad today. I just had a call from my dear friend who is dying. My tears are running down my cheeks and I am beside myself with grief. She is too far away and I cannot be there with her. I don't think either of us wants to be together because we want to be in control of our own memories of happier, healthier times. We talk often but not often enough because she is having trouble breathing. Another freaking loss in my eightieth year. As my mother would say, "and so it goes." I hate that I sound like, "poor me" but if I am being truthful, it is exactly how I feel. Poor me, poor her, poor all of us in the throes of loss.

Poor us,

Me

Can you be grateful for sad tears?

When do you feel like poor me?

Poor Me

June 6, 2024

Dear Betty,

Yesterday the tears just wouldn't stop flowing. I could have been a puddle on the floor. I don't think that I have ever felt so alone. Anchors kept occupying my thoughts. It seems that the closest I could come to identifying my feelings was one an image of anchors being cut off from a fishing boat in the middle of a muddy looking lake. All of my anchors, the ones that keep me grounded and not drifting about aimlessly. The ones that told me the truth, encouraged me, admonished me but most of all loved me seem to be out of my reach. Who will keep me from drifting off needlessly into my own abstract idea of the answer to what now?

All of this came to me because I talked to my dear, dear friend who is dying. She called yesterday and I could hear through the phone line or whatever it is that transmits phone messages in this age, how frail she has become. I could hear her pain. Because I think that I can always fix all, do all, be all, I felt defeated. Still, at least I can be with her in this way and I can still hear her voice. So much loss in this year of my life. Today I can write to you Betty and I am thankful for that. I am not feeling so much "poor me" as yesterday but rather grateful that I am able to process my thoughts and feelings more truthfully.

About that, truthfully, one of my poor me thoughts yesterday or maybe it was just an authentic thought for a woman of an age was...how long will it be before it is me saying goodbye?

Only slightly poor me,

Me

Who or what are the anchors for you?

What might you do to process your "poor me" times?

Out of the Cocoon

June 8, 2024

Dear Betty,

I have discovered that there are just too many days on my calendar that remain blank. And so, I decided that it was time to do something about that. Yesterday I stepped out of my comfy cocoon and joined the Senior Travel Club of Walworth County. Now Betty, you might think, "what is the big deal about that?" Well, you see underneath all of my past bravado there is still a little girl nervous about going to the first day of school.

I bravely walked into the meeting room not really knowing what to expect. There were a lot of people there. I was greeted at the door and asked to sign in. I explained that I was not a member but that I wanted to be a member. The woman gave me a badge that said, "Guest" and directed me to take a seat. I tried to explain again that even though I was a guest I did want to become a member. "Just take a seat," she said and I obeyed. At the table that I chose was a woman named Sandy. She was so helpful, made me feel welcome and comfortable, and helped me complete the form that would make me a member. She delivered it to the appropriate person and came back with my receipt and then proceeded to tell me that as a member I would receive a new badge next month with my name on it.

So, Betty, I am now a member of the travel club and I have been named. Driving home I felt proud of myself for stepping out into the abyss of senior life. I am not at all sure that I have found my tribe. In fact, I don't think this is it but no matter what they are, I am sure it will be fun to travel with them and time will tell.

Traveling?

Me

What are the cocoons that keep you from breaking free and growing?

Have you ever felt that something was good but just not for you?

How do you feel about not doing something just because someone thinks you should?

In Defense of Selfing

June 8, 2024

Dear Betty,

In the book *Grace in Aging*, the author Kathleen Dowling Singh writes about "selfing." She tells us that if we have developed a habit of selfing we cannot be open to each awareness that comes to us in our mindfulness. I find that it has taken me some amount of time to develop the habit of selfing. That to be self-aware gives me the foundation to explore all of the other aspects of my life. If I am not self-aware then who am I? Perhaps I am a living stereotype going through the motions of what we have been led to believe our lives should be at seventy, eighty, and beyond.

One of my recent perceptions is this: I enjoy being alone, but I do not like doing things alone. Here in my comfortable cocoon, I can say that I am truly comfortable. I like the quiet sometimes and I like filling my space with music or an interesting talk show or maybe an interesting book that I can listen to on my tablet. When thinking about leaving my comfortable space, I now realize that I find it more enjoyable or at least comfortable to be out and about with another person or persons. I am trying to stretch my "alone muscles" by going out and about by myself. I will let you know if this turns out to be healthy selfing or not.

The thought of it has for sure helped me realize just how much of my life was spent with others.

Selfing,

Me

Do you ever feel like you need to stretch your "alone muscles"?

How do you feel about selfing?

What do you think about being self-aware?

Energy Meets Expectations

June 9, 2024

Dear Betty,

Remember when I talked about my energy level not meeting my expectations? Well, I spent today in the reality of that statement. I went to bed thinking that I would go to church this morning. This morning came and I just couldn't get myself together enough to go to church. Actually, I don't want to do much of anything today. It has been a busy couple of days and obviously my energy level has sunk to some low level that I believe I will have to get used to as we progress through this year and beyond. I don't feel guilty about not going to church or about choosing to just do whatever comes along today even if that means sitting on the porch enjoying the sunshine or taking an afternoon nap. I like this part of eighty.

Does it make sense to think that maybe the statement or question should be; is my reality meeting my expectations? This would have me understand that I need to have expectations. The more I continue to explore my life at eighty the more I realize that my expectations throughout my life have been pretty simple. I also realize that I never fit the mold of "what I should be doing or who I should be." Why would I change that now?

Ah, a new awareness. Perhaps this contradicts the idea of vision boards or putting the words about the things that you want to manifest out into the universe. Creating a vision board or practicing daily mantras are ways we make our expectations concrete. I find that if I start obsessing about my future, the rest of my days and of course my death, I forget to stay grounded in the present moment and that frightens me. For whatever time I have left, I want to try, notice that I am saying *try* Betty, to be present to each day. That just reminded me of the postal service's old saying, "Neither rain nor sleet nor dead of winter shall keep me from..." I might say neither rain nor snow nor dead of night will keep me from experiencing the love around me, the beauty around me and even the grief and loss that at times overwhelms me.

"All is well and all manner of things will be well."

– Julian of Norwich

Porch–sitting,

Me

Does your energy level meet your expectations?

How do you feel when you make the choice to trust your instincts about your energy, even if this conflicts with your expectations?

Presence, Awareness, and Identity

June 10, 2024

Dear Betty, Do you think that people who live by following their intuition are unsettled because they do not follow a prescribed plan? My ponder this morning took me to the idea that my life would have followed a much tidier path if I had a plan. I was never one to fall into fads or belong to clicks. Instead, I lived life by putting one foot in front of the other and at times throwing caution to the wind. At times, it was challenging, even scary. Given the man that I was married to I don't think we could have done it any differently.

Perhaps my daily journey now would be less oblique if I prescribed a "plan". I don't mean to sound absolutely radical Betty; I do adhere to all of the special holidays. I do try to fall into at least some of the clothing trends. I even find some of them rather kitschy and fun to wear. But I would never say that I fit the norm of what others adopt as active aging, graceful aging, or even the idea that every older person is wise. I am still trying to stay on the path of presence, awareness, and identity. I bet that if I stick to it these things alone will carry me off to my last days. For me, this idea seems better to me than denial, wishful thinking, and living according to someone else's plan.

I do appreciate the many wisdoms available to me from wherever they come. From my great grandchildren or an ism from a complete stranger. Betty, you help me to be a wisdom seeker and finder.

I took the other path,

Me

What does the plan you have created for your life now have as a foundation?

How do you feel about living into someone else's plan for eldering?

Just an Ordinary Day

June 12, 2024

Dear Betty,

It was just an ordinary day. I wonder why I would describe it as "just" an ordinary day. Perhaps because for most of my life I wanted things to not be ordinary. I wanted exciting things to happen, meaningful things, helpful things, or ordered things, but not ordinary.

Today, I went to the dentist, did all of the morning things like care for the dog, make the bed, and you know the rest, ordinary things. After the dentist I didn't feel like "just" going home to do nothing in particular. I called Christy and we decided to go to lunch. We could have chosen one of our ordinary places but instead we went to a place that she hadn't been before. I guess that was a little out of the ordinary. The rest of the day was uneventful, ordinary.

Today in my morning reflection I realize that even ordinary days can be good. I got over the stress of going to a new dentist. I made the decision to have a lunch date in the middle of the week. I felt relaxed and satisfied in the evening. I was happy for an ordinary day. So, Betty, I am declaring that ordinary has its benefits too. Maybe I should celebrate the ordinary more often.

At eighty I guess I have decided that if I were to "just" be for a day, or "just" let a day be ordinary I would be missing out on another day of my fleeting life. How silly of me. It would be better for me to accept each day as a gift and an opportunity to see the world around me, to experience a spontaneous moment and to enjoy the company of my daughter doing a not-so-ordinary thing.

"Just" Me

When does an ordinary thing become a not-so-ordinary thing?

In what ways do you think ordinary can be something to celebrate?

Bits and Pieces of My Heart

June 14, 2024

Dear Betty,

My best friend died last night at 7:00 p.m. I am missing her already, even though we lived on two sides of the country, we still stayed in touch, talked often, and shared so many really fine memories. I am really starting to feel the isolation of old age. So many losses, too many loved ones have left the planet. Still, I have so much to be grateful for: my family, new friends, and my health.

It seems like I am losing bits and pieces of my heart. Or perhaps I should think instead that those I love, have loved, are resting right here in a special place in my heart. Yesterday, very early in the morning just as day was breaking, I saw a partial rainbow out of my west window. I am sure it was a sign sent to prepare me for the loss of Dre. Or maybe it was a sign of hope for all of those who have left me and for me as well to carry on. I realize that I have not been paying attention to the gifts that I am sure have crossed my path, like the rainbow. I hope to be more attentive soon.

Sad & Hopeful,

Me

How can we collect the bits and pieces of our hearts?

What signs in nature can you take into your heart when you are feeling lost and alone?

Voices

June 15, 2024

Dear Betty,

Some days I wake feeling empty. I wonder what I should do to fill the empty space. Then, I think, maybe I should just let it be and experience the emptiness. I don't like this feeling. It is like a large cavity in the middle of my being that I don't think will ever be filled again. I am woefully sad and long for the presence of those who have been so much a part of my life, of me.

When things happen to me like the loss of my dear friend, it is then that I wish that Don was still here with me, I want to hope that he can hear me as I cry out; I am so alone. I know that I cannot call Dre whenever I want to, I will never hear her lovely, sexy voice again. I want to hear his voice as well. I want his comforting arms around me.

Grace has been a blessed gift through this long life. It is that grace that will see me through. It is the grace of knowing that lets me rest in the love that is left me from each of those who have died and left me empty but still longing for whatever may be waiting for me on the long path of my life's journey.

If feeling empty is a sign that I have loved and been loved, then I will be empty today knowing that tomorrow will be another day. I celebrate the love that was Don and Dre, and Tom. Sometime it will be my turn to sleep the long sleep of death but not just yet.

Be filled,

Me

Are there voices that you long to hear?

What do you long to say to someone that you miss today?

What fills you when you are feeling empty?

Destination Unknown

June 16, 2024

Dear Betty,

Here is my description of my eightieth year to date; being eighty is like standing on the platform of a train station waiting for a train whose destination is unknown.

Each day I try to focus on what I am thinking and what I am feeling. Some days are silver and some gold but most are a conundrum. I enjoy the days that make sense to me, the ones that are clear and offer a vision or at least something that resembles my current reality. As I pursue meaning for my life now, something that I can share with you Betty, I realize that I am determined and most days I am able to find some focus and reason for this exercise. I will try my best to be faithful to you Betty.

On another note, this morning as I was reflecting on the sad truth of the many losses at this stage of life, I remembered my mother saying in her late years, "All my people are gone. There is no one left to talk to about old times."

I am sure that she knew the feeling of loneliness but she did not ever act on it. She was more likely to share how she felt about the losses in her life.

As she often said, "And so it goes."

And so it goes today,

Me

How do you feel about the analogy of being at the train station, destination unknown?

What does "and so it goes" mean to you?

Raised Eyebrows

June 17, 2024

Dear Betty,

Since the recent loss of my dear friend Dre, I have been counting the things that I seem to be missing on this year's journey. I miss Don's voice but more than his voice I miss his "looks". The look he might give me if he thought that I had said something that I shouldn't or the look he might give me when he agreed with me, or the times when our eyes would meet in a crowded room meaning "I am here with you."

In my life I have spent a good amount of time encouraging women to find their own voices. This meant I encouraged them to come to some understanding of who they were and what they were about. I tried to allow them the space to say what was on their minds and hearts. Now as I think about voices, I can say that I can still hear my mother's voice and my father's laugh. I can hear Auntie Margaret's laugh and Aunt Tree's raised eyebrows when she told her very unlikely stories. Dre had a very distinctive voice and a particular way of speaking. I will miss that terribly, especially when I do not receive a phone call that starts, "Hi hon, it's Dre."

As I continue this journey through my eightieth year I want to pay more attention to the voices. The voices of others and what they are really saying and my own voice and how I perceive how others are hearing me. It is more than remembering the sound of a voice, it is what is or has been said behind the words that give volume to the voice.

Listening,

Me

Have you ever received one of "those" looks?

What voices are you most likely to listen to?

How do you perceive the way others listen to you?

How do you want others to hear your voice?

Stay the Course

June 18, 2024

Dear Betty,

In one of my awakenings during the night, I thought about the phrase "stay the course". What is my course I wondered? Do I even have one? So, I have learned that the definition of the phrase we are most familiar with means to continue with a process, effort, etc. even though it is difficult. To stay in the 1800s definition also means to stop something. I could go on and on with this but suffice it to say that I have accepted the challenge to continue with the process I have begun that is writing to you Betty.

Today, I learned that another one of my close friends is entering hospice. This news brought me back to my image of standing on the train platform waiting for a train without knowing the destination. Too many of my family and friends are getting on the train. It is time to get their ticket punched. Here I stand, still waiting. Mind you Betty, I am not in a hurry to get on that train but I am way too aware of the many losses that are to be endured as we begin the year of eighty.

So much sadness, loneliness, and other emotions that I am not as yet able to express. I will however stay the course and try, you see, I said *try* to take each day as it comes. Let me be grateful for what each day brings me, for my health and especially for my family. It is for you,

Betty, and for them that I will do my best to stay the course and I promise that I will not "stay" the course before it has run its course.

Waiting while grieving,

Me

How do you feel about the phrase "stay the course"?

What is the course that you might set for yourself?

Rear-View Mirror

June 19, 2024

Dear Betty,

Eighty is a rear–view mirror. Pictures, experiences, people appear behind me and still these pictures remind me of the good productive life that I have enjoyed. At times though I can get caught up in the rear–view mirror. It seems even though some of the pictures, or memories of some experiences or people, may not be the happiest. Sometimes looking back can even bring feelings of regret, hurt, or disappointment. I wish that I would have done something differently or responded in ways that were more appropriate or kind.

There are days that if left to my own vices, I would only look back because looking at what is before me is just too overwhelming. The future never daunted me. I guess I have always relied on my ability to deal with whatever came along. This is no longer available to me; the reality is that I am sure that the day is coming that I will have to rely on others to help me make decisions for me. Decisions that I have no way of understanding today. I am just not there yet.

What is the answer, Betty? Do I take pleasure in the rear–view mirror and continue to lead my comme ci, comme ça life or should I be more pro–active about my future? Actually, I am proud of myself. I have made plans for my demise and I have shared my wishes for my even older age. I guess what I cannot share is what each new day will bring, the unexpected that is sure to happen.

I saw a sign once that said, "Don't look back, you are not going that way." At eighty the thought that one should not look back means the absence of all of the life that has come before. The wisdom shared, the love given, the many benefits of friendships, the pride of accomplishment and so much more. If I stop looking back, I will not enjoy the comfort of loving smiles, good times, and the bittersweet loss of my loved one. In some strange way his spirit lives on when I am brave enough to look into the rear-view mirror. Each day becomes another image for me to view in my mirror tomorrow with gratitude.

Looking back moving forward,

Me

What do you see in your rear-view mirror?

How does what you see in your rear-view mirror inform how you feel today?

Hoping and Wishing

June 20, 2024

Dear Betty,

Eighty is like being an old battery-operated clock watching the time tick, tick by and hoping that it is not yet time to replace the battery.

Do we live in hope or is it a kind of anticipation that we want to call hope because then the clock is still ticking? I want to anticipate that the clock will keep on ticking for some time yet but still I look to the future of this eightieth year with some kind of realistic view, I hope.

Can we talk about hope without talking about wish? I mean the difference is this: I want hope to be positive, I want my hopes to be filled with goodness. When I think about wishes, I think about birthday cakes and candles and making a wish. But I also think about the phrase "I wish" in relation to or at times feeling like regret. I wish I would have handled that differently, or I wish I would have been more present or loving or kind.

Betty, do you think that maybe my hope for the future is more about having my wish for being present or loving or kind come true, than my need to want my future whatever that may be to be peaceful, calm, and graceful?

Well Betty, it seems like I have more work to do with the words hope, wish, and grace. Or maybe I should just hope that I will recognize them when they appear again in this most interesting and challenging year.

I wish,

Me

Do you think that hope and wish are related?

What are some of your fondest wishes in these eldering years?

How do you experience hope these days?

Morbs

June 22, 2024

Dear Betty,

Once again, I find myself suffering from a case of the morbs. The old Victorian word for melancholy, sadness, and grief. It has only been one week since my dear friend died. I miss her deep down in my soul. I keep thinking that I want to call her and tell her how sad I am and how much she helped me along my grieving journey since Don died. We always had so much to share.

It is a weird day weather-wise. It was cloudy this morning and very humid and hot. We just had a downpour and now it seems that the sky is just blue gray. I keep looking toward the west hoping to see another Dre rainbow. Not there today, no signs at all.

I will just have to rely on my memory today, Betty, to hear their voices and the reassurance that they always brought to me. They have been grace in my life. Once again, I have been thinking about how I thought that people in their seventies or eighties were really old. Now I rail against the thought that they were only in their eighties. Not old at all. What does any age feel like after all? I don't think I feel an age, it just is what it is. I am more concerned with how I feel and what I think and how I am meant to relate at eighty.

Youngish,

Me

*Do you have a word for times when you are feeling sad
or melancholy?*

What does any age feel like?

Do-Overs

June 24, 2024

Dear Betty,

Do-overs. Sometimes I wish I could do over bits and pieces of my life. Then I realize that the outcome might not be any different. Things will happen, opportunities may be taken advantage of or lost, families change, the world changes and in the end, I continue to age. Oh yes Betty, there certainly are things I wish I could take back. Conversations that I have had or work that I have done that I may not have been as centered or as focused as I might have been. Perhaps I took things a bit too personally. I know that I have mellowed some in my last decade.

Do-overs. If there are things that I wish I could do over it would be spending more time engaged fully in present moments. Of course, spending more of this decade with Don. Conversations that for whatever reason never quite reached a conclusion. That old clock just keeps ticking away and before you realize it you are eighty. My hope is that I can remain awake and aware of each day ahead while remembering with joy and gratitude the days and times long gone and that I have left behind.

Doing now,

Me

Are there times or experiences that you wish you could do-over?

How different do you think they might be?

Upside-Down Cake

June 25, 2024

Dear Betty,

Sometimes I think that my life is made up of circumstances that I might describe as being an upside-down cake. I begin a day or a task by putting in all of the ingredients. Checking to make sure the container will be the right size, is there enough sugar to make it sweet? Will it have all of the necessary stuff to give it substance? When all is ready, I say, OK lets go! Ready to face the day. Then suddenly, just when I think that I have done it, all is good, the day is almost done, I flip over the pan and guess what Betty, what should have been the pretty side of the cake doesn't come out of the pan as it should and it is a crumbled mess. Some days are just like that.

When life turns you upside down, just take a bite out of it anyway.

Off to do the ordinary things today: bank, pharmacy, grocery store. I am not anticipating any upside-down events today, hopefully.

Right side up,

Me

How do you deal with days that turn out like an upside down cake?

What kind of days are upside down for you?

A Quiet Mind

June 27, 2024

Dear Betty,

Full Stop! I found my mind racing today. Not toward any one thing in particular, but rather wondering, planning, and remembering. Why is it so difficult at times to quiet my mind? Could it be that I just like to have things in order? If my mind would just settle on one thing that might be construed as focus. Like...if I spent time wondering about a book that I read or am reading or if I am planning an outing, knowing when and where to would be helpful. Remembering can be a pleasant experience that at times can even make me smile. Certainly, if I spend time thinking about what is concerning me the conclusion might be to make a decision about how to remedy my concern.

I need to remember to take "Full Stop" moments. Stop, take a breath, watch the birds landing in the bird tree or listen to the old frog in the pond. I think this is easier said than done, but worth some effort. Betty, why should this be so hard? Ah ha, because it involves feelings. If I could really come to a full stop, I might feel sad or guilty or alone or back to drifting unanchored in the waters of this eightieth year.

Full Stop! I think that I will give it a try. I have no idea how successful I might be but if I can do it even for a minute or two, I might find the exercise pleasant and then let it happen more naturally. Maybe it will bring me to a kind and meaningful reverie. Maybe it will even create a space in which all of the other thoughts and feelings will make more sense. Maybe I will find them not quite so daunting, doable even.

Stopped,

Me

How comfortable are you with being quiet?

What does a quiet mind sound like to you?

What keeps you from finding time for your own journey into the quiet place of your mind?

Signs and Wonders

June 28, 2024

Dear Betty,

Signs and wonders. Do you believe that if we are willing to pay attention and look for them, we can find signs all around us that can help us to answer the questions swirling around our searching minds? The day Dre died, I looked to the western sky. It was morning and I was just doing the ordinary thing of letting York out for his morning constitutional. The sky seemed to be divided into sections. To the south it was blue with puffy clouds floating gently but not really going anywhere. To the north, the sky was dark and foreboding the way it is when rain is on its way. However, there in the gray cloudless western sky I saw a partial rainbow. I thought this was strange, as there are rainbows here on the farm often, but they are usually in the eastern sky and almost always full bending from one end of the farm to the other. Dre lived in Oregon, the far West.

Later that day I learned that Dre had died. I truly believe that the rainbow was a sign that her second journey was going to happen soon. Betty, I know that she would believe it was a sign as well. I know that she had that kind of spirituality. It was one of the things that I loved about her.

I haven't seen a rainbow since but I have noticed the clouds these days and watched them for some time with wonder. Have you ever looked at the sky and the clouds and created pictures in them? One of the signs and wonders that I want to hold on to today are twofold. I will always remember what I have come to call "Dre's rainbow."

I want to believe that Don sent me a sign in the early evening clouds the other day. I found several clouds that looked like they had heart shapes in them. They were there and then they moved gently away and became something else. Betty, I am not sure exactly what that means but I will continue to look up, hoping for more signs and wonders with a smile on my face because looking to the heavens with a prayer in my heart is wonderful.

Seeking,

Me

How do signs and wonders appear for you?

When did we stop looking for signs and wonders?

What would you think or feel if you tried again to find them?

The Far Reaches of My Absent Mind

June 29, 2024

Dear Betty,

There is something that I am becoming very aware of. There are so many things that I find absent these days. It makes me think about my life in one of its earlier stages. So many things to occupy my time, responsibilities, deadlines, planning, caring, and more. Oh yes, I do have responsibilities now but they are small by comparison. I do not really have deadlines unless you count being on time for a lunch date with a friend. I am not doing much planning because I am still trying to figure out what it is I should be planning for. I have taken care of all of the major things that will occur in the future and the small things will be managed as they appear. I hope to never stop caring about so many things.

Now for the other side of absenteeism. The person that I spend more than half of my life with is absent. My dearest friend is absent. Traveling with my travel friend is absent. My faith in our country and its leaders is pretty close to being absent. I am concerned about my lack of ambition to be creative. I guess my ambition is absent. Making meals is a different kind of absence. I, of course, still cook for myself but the joy of it, yep, pretty much absent.

Betty, do you think it is healthy, you know mentally, emotionally, to name the absences in my life? As I write to you today, I wonder if I am creating a downer? Still, if I am trying to name this eightieth year journey I have to be truthful and realistic. There are things in my life now that are absent and I do miss some of them. Others to my way of thinking are just noticed so that I might decide to leave them be or to try to get them back. Maybe new things will arrive on this journey to fill the absent space. Who knows?

Absent or not?

Me

How have you named the absences in your life?

What will you do to fill the empty spaces?

Prescription for Aging

June 29, 2024

Dear Betty.

There is no prescription for life at eighty. Each journey is a unique venture into the "wherever" and "whatever" lies ahead.

The other day I had lunch with a good friend. She is also trying to traverse her eighties with a modicum of grace and understanding. I wish there was a prescription for life at eighty. If there is one, I have not yet found it. I have spent way too much money on books hoping for the answers that will equip me for now. I have concluded that indeed there is no prescription, just a re-arranging of the same self-help ideas that are the basis of most of the current literary endeavors that have been the bread and butter of modern-day self-help gurus. The closest I have come to anything that I can grab onto are some of the writers like May Sarton, long gone now, but who wrote of her life at seventy. Perhaps reading someone's journals or diaries would present a clue or maybe a lesson that could be held onto while trying to discover one's own journey.

OK Betty, I confess I have just told you of one of my biases. In my defense, though, I will say that it is frustrating to go to book after book and article after article without finding at least one "ah ha" moment. The best I could do to help my friend was to once again encourage her to accept her own journey, view it as a unique venture that is hers alone. Still, it is reassuring to know that others are struggling or at least questioning the same things that anyone is aware of, or who has hopes that being eighty is meaningful and perhaps even joyful or at the very least Betty, happy.

If you should find the elusive prescription Betty, please share it with me. I would be most grateful.

Asking for a friend,

Me

Do you have a prescription for life at sixty, seventy, or eighty? How would you describe it?

What will your elder journey mean to others?

July

Life is a Scrabble

July 1, 2024

Dear Betty,

Life at eighty is a scrabble board of beliefs and nonbeliefs.

Some days I wonder if I still believe what I used to believe yesterday. How has my belief system changed? I find that if I were to really think about the things that I would put into the unbelief space on the Scrabble board, there might be several other words that might fill the spaces under it. Which words would create the most other words? Would there be more words in my spaces around what I believe?

What am I talking about Betty? Are there things in my thoughts or my value system that I used to believe, that now I'm not sure about? I used to believe that the world was a wonderful place and that all people on the planet had the potential to be good, honest, caring and capable of love. Today I am afraid to say that there are some categories of my fellow worldly inhabitants that I have placed in the unbelief space or that I feel rather dubious about.

One of Don's definitions of belief was: if you go out to start the car you believe that when you start the car it will start. Following his logic today I am not sure that I believe that the car will start. What if it was not assembled properly and when I turn the key it will blow up? There are some things happening in our lives and in our world today that I no longer feel worthy of my belief in them. I am not sure that I have total unbelief since I tend to be a glass half full kind of a gal. Let's just say Betty, that I have lost a lot of confidence in more things than I would like to admit.

I do still believe that I have love in my life, I have faith, I have people around me that I put my trust in so I guess that qualifies as belief. My unbelief in the more nebulous things at this life stage scare me at times. I guess that the way to escape the fear and foreboding is to take each day as it comes and to hold onto my beliefs because they are stronger than the unbeliefs.

As my mom would say, "and so it goes."

Me

What are the core words on the scrabble board of your life?

How do you feel about the unbelief spaces, will you fill them?

Independent

July 4, 2024

Dear Betty,

The family gathered. Good food was shared. Neighbors invited. Fireworks happened, the first in a couple of years. They were wonderful. The fireworks crew did a marvelous job. A good time was had by all.

The best part of this story however is what happened before the fireworks and while the family was gathered and waiting. Jake surprised us all with a bottle of whiskey that he had distilled in Nebraska. It was made from our home-grown corn. The bottle has a picture of Don on it and it says Papa's Whiskey.

Of course, there were tears all around and a toast made with the special vintage.

If only. How many times do I think about this these days? We just have to live each day with intent and just the right amount of stoicism. Know that it is really OK to have "if only" moments. They remind us of what we hold dear and meaningful in our lives.

Independent,

Me

Do you have a sense of independence? What does it feel like?

What is your definition of independence as an elder?

A Page Turned

July 5, 2024

Dear Betty,

Life at eighty is turning the page to another chapter without knowing the name of the book.

What might the name of the book be? Maybe something like: When did eighty arrive? Who cares if I am old? Oh, shit, I am old. I could probably go on and on but I think I will settle with where I started: Dear Betty at eighty.

Does it really matter if we know the name of the book that is us? I think it helps if we are serious about turning the page with some intention of awareness. Having a title or direction does help me to keep plugging away in my search for what this chapter and the one after and the one after that means. What will the end of the story or the book be for me Betty?

I just don't know what the rest of this eightieth year will bring or how I may be changed because of it. I do know that already in the previous chapters of this year I find myself more diligent about being present to who is and what is happening around me. I certainly realize that my body is starting to show signs of wear. Betty, one of the hard chapters in this book of mine is the forever-after sadness that has become part of my being. No matter how you cut the eightieth birthday cake, know that one of the things to be faced in this chapter is loss and change. No changing that truth. It just is what it is.

Read on,

Me

What do you think might be the title of your book of life?

Can you name the issues that you are facing at this time of life?

A Little Silliness Soothes the Soul

July 6, 2024

Dear Betty,

We remember the times when we were brave enough to be silly, wearing costumes and playing silly games. Times when those who would never think of acting in silliness break down and become the life of the party. Ah, those were the days.

It was a grand fourth of July. Warm enough to be outside and let the little ones play in the water of their tiny pool but cool enough to be comfortable for the adults who sat outside and watched the little ones play and at times act silly.

I wondered when we all got too old to act a little silly? Where was the spontaneity of the past? When did the boys turn into men who would rather sit on the deck and tell one man ship stories? Why did no one get thrown into the pond?

Aunt Tree was great at being silly. She was often scoffed at by the other relatives but I thought she was the one I wanted to emulate. She knew how to have fun, play dress up for parties, and tell great stories. I think I will try to be more like her in the future, now in my eightieth year. Perhaps people will just expect me to act this way. They will excuse my behavior because after all, I am old.

Soothing my soul with silliness,

Me

When was the last time you let yourself be silly?

How do you feel about being spontaneous?

The Party is Over

July 7, 2024

Dear Betty,

The last day of the fourth of July weekend. Tomorrow we slip back into the everyday routine. I wonder how we might hold on to just a little of the feeling of going slow, less stress, playful moments, and remembering what the holiday was all about after all.

For one on this part of the journey who is still trying to find routine, the day after is just the day after. The usual things of daily life are becoming routine again. It is my approach to them that has changed. I have been quite an ordered person. Laundry on Monday, errands on Tuesday etc. Now, however, I have greater freedom when I do my routine things. Sometimes I do laundry on Thursday and errands on Monday or when they are called for. In the beginning of this year, it felt rather strange, almost naughty to break the routine rules. Now it at times makes me smile.

For now the party is over but the memory has been made. I think I will try to engage more in memory-making than in sticking to a routine. Because I do have the gift of choice and I like where my eighty challenge is taking me, most days anyway.

After the party,

Me

How do you feel when the party is over?

What routines do you find helpful?

*What do you think about the idea of memory making,
letting yourself break from set routines?*

History Repeats Itself

July 14, 2024

Dear Betty,

Feeling really tired today. Had a nice but short vacation and came back to the news that the Republican Candidate for President was a target of an assassination attempt. He is OK.

More important to me is the news that my friend is in end stage COPD. So how am I feeling? Frustrated, surprised, and deep down, sad. Life at this stage is always full of a variety of losses. Still the ones that sink you right down to your toes are the all too often loss of those we love and our dear friends.

Betty, we cannot help but ask ourselves those recurring questions. You know the ones that ask, "Did I do enough?" "Was I present enough?" "What could I have done differently?" "Did I love enough?" "Was I a good friend?" This self-reflection is also an ongoing part of life at eighty but this year has been too much of a reminder of too many things that until now were easy to put on the back burner. Now they are soundly on the front burner and I can no longer ignore them if I want to continue my journey of authenticity and presence here and now in the time that is mine.

Sadly,

Me

What are the recurring questions that you ask yourself?

How about all of the other kinds of losses we can't help but come face to face with from middle age forward?

What are some back burner losses that you are ready to move to the forefront?

Clock Work

July 5, 2024

Dear Betty,

Betty, do you remember the time of our lives when things seemed to work out just like clockwork? There were certain tasks that happened during the week. Monday through Friday meant work and school and meetings that let the community know that you were well meaning and involved in it because that is what was expected of adults, families, neighbors. Weekends were set aside for at-home tasks, church, birthday celebrations, picnics or vacations and visiting relatives. That is what was expected of me growing up and because it was what I thought was "the way" it is how I began my adult years.

I don't know exactly when I found out that I could do things differently. I found myself questioning the old clockwork ways. I had a partner that helped me understand and enjoy the meaning of spontaneity. Our views on raising children and volunteering were out of the norm as well.

Needless to say, our decision to challenge the clockwork ways of our generation were not always met with open arms or minds. I find myself now slipping back into just a bit of a clockwork mentally. Remember, Betty, I said just a bit. I still enjoy those spontaneous moments or saying yes when the old me, not the literal old me, the other one wants to say no. A firm yes at times feels so good and is usually rewarded with a kind of quiet peace of mind.

Saying yes more than no,

Me

Do you think that you have clockwork mentally?

What would have to change for you to react differently now?

How do you feel about saying yes when the old clockwork tapes want you to say no?

Dying Has Given Me Purpose

July 16, 2024

Dear Betty,

Yesterday I visited a dear friend of mine who is dying. She is in hospice at home. As we talked about memories of all of the years we shared and the many adventures that we had together; she said, "Dying has given me purpose." What an interesting thing to say, I thought. "What does that mean?" I asked.

She said, "Well, I have to think about all of the things that need to be taken care of, who needs to be notified, telling my boys where to find things and what they have to do to take care of my business affairs. So many details to deal with."

Just as there is no prescription for life at eighty Betty, there is no prescription for how each of us ventures into death either. I will think about this visit many times in the future.

My friend's life did insist that she take care of things. She was a single mom with three boys. She suffered the loss of a husband early in their lives. She divorced her second husband and began a very successful business in the financial world. Her life took her on many ventures: teacher, artist, mother, grandmother, friend, and business woman. So, Betty, why would she not approach this journey any differently?

She sought purpose throughout her life, and I am happy that she knows it now.

Humbled,

Me

How do you feel about the statement "Dying has given me purpose"?

Do you think that her need to take care of things is part of how a cultural generation of elders approaches their end times?

If Wishes Were Horses

July 19, 2024

Dear Betty,

Today I find myself weary. I so want the happy days back. I would even settle for new happy days. It seems that the first one half of my eightieth year has held little happy and a lot of sad. Perhaps this is the lesson. Life past eighty is imbued with loss countered by hopes of better days.

My mother used to say, "If wishes were horses, beggars would ride."

"If wishes were horses, beggars would ride" is a proverb and nursery rhyme, first recorded about 1628 in a collection of Scottish proverbs, which suggests if wishing could make things happen, then even the most destitute people would have everything they wanted.

Do you think those of us destitute of hope and without wishes could take this as a challenge to check our attitudes? Try to understand why we are destitute and rather accept it as our destiny at eighty or invoke the deeper resource within ourselves and grab onto the positive surprises of life that I am sure still cross our threshold.

Still wishing,

Me

Have you ever heard this proverb before?

How do you experience your wishes, hopes, or your attitudes about them?

What are some of the positive surprises that have crossed your path lately?

Never Stop Seeking

July 22, 2024

Dear Betty,

I went to church yesterday. I had some idea that something magical would happen. I hoped for a word or a lesson or a comment that would help me out of the funk I seem to find myself in these days. Feeling mildly depressed and very sad, I encouraged myself to get up, put on some suitable church clothes and make the effort.

Well Betty there were no magic bullets, no ah ha moment. What I did find however, was a picture of grace and faith. The man, Thomas, was sitting in front of me. It was so clear to me that he is a man of deep faith. It was something about the way he bowed his head, the way he responded to the prayers asked of him by the priest and the kind way he turned to me and asked my name. It was worth it Betty.

Worth it to make the effort and to find in this simple elder man a sample of what I think I was looking for in the end. Perhaps we just don't always "feel" it but there is something in me that keeps calling me back to the faith of my youth. The time when I believed, boy did I believe. I am reaching back to those times experiencing the "feeling" in my memory. It may not be long when I will just "feel" them in the present and in the future as I continue to wend my way through eighty.

Faithfully,

Me

Have you ever had a "Thomas" experience?

What is deep inside of you that keeps calling you back to something from your youth?

How will you answer the call?

Magic Happens When It Happens

July 23, 2024

Dear Betty,

Several years ago, I was on a retreat at Mountain Home Lodge in California. On a day that was spent alone and in nature, I was visited by a large mama deer. She was so close to me that I thought I should have been startled but I was not. I greeted her and she stood for a minute or maybe two and then quietly moved on. A few minutes later she reappeared with her fawn. Again, I greeted her and thanked her for bringing her baby. Her presence stayed with me all that day and for the rest of the week. What was her message?

Yesterday I was driving into town and from at least a quarter mile away I saw something in the road. I thought it might be a large truck given that there were construction signs near the area where I saw the large object. Lo and behold as I got closer, I realized that it was a very large mama deer. She just stood there and looked at me. A truck coming from the other way stopped as did I. Suddenly she was gone. I do not recall seeing her leave or run into the woods. She was just gone. Well, I thought perhaps I should be paying more attention to the magic in my world, right here on my lowly country road.

I decided that I should take a look at my daily reading and to my surprise it said, "My soul thirsts for God." The scripture in Psalm 42:1 tells us "As a deer thirst for streams so water, so we should thirst for God." – Bible Gateway

Betty, don't you think that this is more than serendipity? I will confess that lately I have not been so happy with God. I seem to be spending most of my eightieth year depressed because of all of the loss experienced. Even though each of my loved ones were deep believers in God, even though I do believe that God answered my prayers when Don was dying, I have been absent from my encounter with her. But, now, I must accept the fact that my lady deer arrived in my psyche just when I needed her. Thank you, God, and thank you mama deer.

Feeling the magic,

Me

Have you ever just longed for a little magic in your life?

When magic happens right in front of you will you accept it?

How will you let yourself be open to the magic of these awesome older years?

The Empty Chair

July 24, 2024

Dear Betty,

Today I am waiting for word that another of my dear friends has died. I continue to add notches on the belt of my life. These are not the kind of notches I want to add.

Somehow, the image of an empty chair comes to me today. In our family we have almost always had designated chairs to sit on at the table. There was also dad's chair, mom's chair, and the company chair in our living room and no child was ever allowed to sit on one of these chairs unless invited.

Don had his chair at the table and to the right of his was the chair for the oldest grandson. Sometimes another one of the boys was allowed to sit there. They called it the bopping chair because Papa would give them a little bop on the head if they misbehaved.

Now I find myself sitting alone at the table, wishing that the empty chairs were filled with all those who have moved on to another table and another chair all their own. Sometimes I don't eat at the table, sitting there on my chair feels somehow just not right. At other times, I sit on my chair and take some moments to remember all that has happened around the table: the laughter, the conversation and the love.

Filling the empty chair,

Me

How do you experience empty chairs in your life?

What are some of the memories that you have about sitting around a table or in a living room or maybe with family on the front porch?

Settle

July 25, 2024

Dear Betty,

Sometimes words just bounce around in my head. They look like word puzzles floating around in midair. Today's word is settled. I thought, "this says a lot about what I am hoping for in this my eightieth year".

I wonder when I will feel settled. You know, Betty, at ease with myself, where I am in the aging process, who I am becoming, all that stuff that we are supposed to be about according to the "experts". What does it mean to be settled? Maybe at ease means comfortable and at a place when I think I have more answers than questions and that the questions are answered more quickly or just put aside because they are just not the most important thing on my mind any given day.

What do I settle for? I settle for less coffee, less judgment about what the youngers are about, and listening to the same story that I have heard before. What I wish I didn't and won't settle for is what I see happening in our communities and world today. I won't settle for the rudeness allowed by those who are examples to our youngers. I won't settle for the loss of decorum and civility by those in power in our highest offices.

If I won't settle, what are my options? I struggle with this always. Now I have come to the conclusion that all I can do is be my best self and when I can, point out my unsettles with whoever will listen. Words do matter and I need to use mine.

Working on being settled,

Me

What unsettles you?

What are some things that you will not settle for?

How do you feel about sharing your unsettles with anyone who will listen?

At a Loss Today

July 27, 2024

Dear Betty,

Another loss. My dear friend of 30 years died two days ago. I knew this was coming. I visited her last week. She was in-home hospice. The first day I saw her, we were able to share stories about all of the things we had done together and the places we had traveled together. We called them our little adventures as most of them were just day trips but always with lunch at a pub if possible. The last time I saw her, she was barely able to answer questions with one word.

And so, I am reminded that my own journey is precarious at best. I am continually faced with loss these days. Too many losses. Still, I will admit that since I have been blessed with eighty years, I knew that loss would be one of the items to be punched on my life ticket. It does not make it any easier but Betty, it does look very different at this stage than when I was a younger. Life was full and loss was not on the horizon. Then it started to creep up slowly and now it is here in full force. There is loss, there is sadness, and there is still life to live.

Getting on with it,

Me

What are the differences in how we viewed loss as youngers and not as we have become olders?

What other losses have you noticed punched on your life ticket?

GONE

July 28, 2024

Dear Betty,

I apologize for continuing on this theme of loss, sadness, and feeling alone. They are gone. This is a phrase that I find myself coming back to often. It seems to bring me back to the present, to my own reality. Still, what does gone mean? At times I think that when I say to myself, "they are gone," I am rash, almost angry. Maybe I am, darn it. I am certainly not happy that I am on my own without the companionship of those who loved me and who told me the truth about myself, who grew me to the woman I am now even if that is alone.

The definition of gone is: "No longer in existence; not part of the present. No longer alive; dead. Ruined." – Merriam-Webster. Betty, it seems harsh to use it in relation to my loved ones. Still, it is true. They are no longer in existence in the same way that I am. They are not part of my present, and they are no longer alive but dead. Any plans that may have been part of the future are ruined.

I want to believe with all of my being Betty, that I will be with them again and that we will all exist in a new reality. Some days, though, it is just too hard to grab onto that hope, that dream. Well, now, I admit that I have had the morbs for the last few days. It is the best way to describe how I am feeling today. It wraps up all of my sadness, loneliness, anger, and disappointment about them being gone.

Feeling a bit low,

Me

How do you cope with the reality that loved ones are gone?

What can you do when you feel like you have morbs?

Do you believe that sharing and telling the truth about how you feel is helpful?

Yes and No

July 28, 2024

Dear Betty,

"No, thank you, not today, rain check?"

"Yes, I would love to, where and what time?"

One of the things that I appreciate about being eighty is my ability or freedom to use the words yes and no in ways that are more truthful than I have ever used them before. For many reasons that I am sure you can imagine Betty, I would say yes when I wanted to say no. I would say no when with just a little encouragement, I might have said yes.

I believe that this new appreciation, the strength of these two little words, are a gift of age. If I in fact do want to proceed through the rest of my life authentically, then I must decide to make choices that are indicative of my true feelings. I do want to be appreciative of the invitations that I may receive but I want my motivation to act on them to be true. It is not my intention to distance myself from others or to have them feel that I am not interested in their company.

Betty, I must try to have my no and my yes be kind. I do not feel that I need to qualify them always, but at times a good reason to say either yes or no can be another way of being honest in a relationship. Ah, here is the wisdom. When giving an answer to a yes or no question, first, listen, then take a moment to give it some thought and then respond with kindness, caring, and good intention.

Then there are some questions that simply require a simple yes or no. Is the sun shining at your house today? Yes. Do you remember how to make your mom's chicken soup? No.

Yes or No, Maybe,

Me

Do you agree with this statement: If you never say yes, what is your no worth? Why or why not?

What has prompted you to say no when you really wanted to say yes?

How do you feel when you trust your intuition and say yes against thoughts of "you should say no"?

Roses Amongst the Garlic

July 29, 2024

Dear Betty,

After several days of wallowing in sadness with a little "woe is me" thrown in, I have returned to the reality that as Don would say, "it is what it is." Why would we when we are in our wonder years think about what the not so wonderful years bring? When life is roses, we don't think about planting garlic.

There are many varieties of roses, Betty, and garlic has healing properties. Back to balance, recognizing the beauty of what life has been and moving gracefully into what it will become. So far, I have found that eighty has brought me some wonderful heirloom roses in dark, luscious velvety colors and textures. Yes, I have planted some garlic along the way. However, I have found that it too is fragrant and colorful in its many uses. I just have to continue to reach deep and find them.

In the garden,

Me

What do you think about the metaphor of roses and garlic?

Do you think you will think about the roses of your life?

Will you appreciate the garlic as well?

AUGUST

Is There Grace in Solitude?

August 1, 2024

Dear Betty,

"I live in that solitude which is painful in youth, but delicious in the years of maturity." – Albert Einstein

I spent a lot of time alone when I was a child. My siblings were grown and gone and my parents were the "speak when you are spoken too" generation. Yes Betty, at times it was painful, this imposed solitude. Still, as I think about it now, I find that there was grace for me in it because I developed a strong imagination. I will confess, Betty, that there were times that my imagination created problems. I heard from my mother more than once, "I don't know where you get these ideas from" At the time, neither did I.

I have been thinking a lot lately about the word grace. There are many definitions and uses for the word. Two that I think come closest to the mark for me are; "do honor or credit to" and "the free and unmerited favor of God." We often say that was a "graced moment." We say grace before a meal, we are graced by someone's presence. I will use grace as identifying a gift in my life. All of that to simply say that as I view solitude now in this gift of years, as a grace. What was painful when I was a child has become this gift. I can easily drift into a state of solitude with little trouble. Does it still stir my imagination? Yes, at times but more often it takes me to reverie and that brings me to gratitude. It can also be just what it is: a time to just be after a life of becoming.

Feeling graced,

Me

What are some of your graced moments?

Do you find grace in these late-in-life years?

How do you feel about finding grace in solitude?

Round Peg in a Square Hole

August 3, 2024

Dear Betty,

I went to a meeting of the travel club yesterday. This was my second time attending a meeting since I joined the club three months ago. Why did I join a travel club you ask? Because I thought that is what people who are eighty are supposed to do. Since I have always been a disciplined and obliging student, friend, wife and mother, I have tried my best to meet the expectations placed on me. I like the way the square peg looks. It is orderly, has clear boundaries and appears to be solid. Just like all of the books I have collected about aging, even doing it gracefully.

Now however, when I try to comply with the rules for aging, I find myself trying to do the ABCs prescribed for a happy life. Back at the meeting I realize that I am not comfortable. So, Betty, I decided to try to figure it out. It is all too sterile, everyone is approximately the same age, size and wearing the same style of clothing. Of the 150 people in the club as near as I can tell only five of them are men.

It reminds me of the many times in my lovely long life that I have tried to be faithful to the ABCs only to find myself being more comfortable with DEF. Thus, as appealing as the square peg is, my round peg does not fit and I am willing to confess that it never will.

Each of us is unique and I don't think that we were designed to be one size fits all humans. I will finish my membership with the travel club this year but I am quite sure that I will not re-up for another attempt at fitting in, or doing what the "book" says. Little by little I am finding that I no longer have the same desire to belong. Perhaps I am getting ever more comfortable in my own skin and my own mind and for sure my ever-changing emotions.

Gladly Round,

Me

Do you see yourself as a round peg or a square peg?

How do you respond to the "what an old person should do" mentality?

What can we learn from the folks who joyfully engage in belonging?

80 is Just a Number

August 3, 2024

Dear Betty,

What is eighty? It is ten more than seventy. They are numbers that help us identify the age of something. In and of themselves they are not magic, do not prescribe a way to live or to be. So, if someone says to you, "act your age" or "for Pete's sake you are eighty years old," remember there is no way to know how one should act their age because it is just a number. When they tell me that for Pete's sake, you are eighty years old, they are trying to tell me how to act out of their own lexicon of how an eighty-year-old should behave. What I think is, "I have lived long enough to be able to act in whatever way I think appropriate, I have earned that right."

Who is Pete anyway?

Getting defensive about my age does not give me permission to ignore someone's caring. Just as a five-year-old mustn't embarrass their parents, so should an elderly grandparent be careful not to embarrass either. It is clear to me that exploring my life journey now in my eightieth year means that I am charting my own course. It doesn't mean that I have a rule book about being eighty or any other age for that matter. It is my own book and I choose when to turn the page on another awareness. If by chance my learnings are helpful to another, then I give thanks for the opportunity to engage in purpose.

Past eighty,

Me

What do you think it means for an older to act their age?

How do you feel about age in general?

Is there a one size fits all when it comes to aging?

Old Hat

August 4, 2024

Dear Betty,

Old fashioned, old news, old hat. I have been thinking about these two little words, "old hat", for some time now. I have come to the conclusion that for me thinking about what is "old hat" has a much different meaning.

Recently I have been invited to join a project with like-minded people who want to start a new group. I like the idea and the energy of those involved. As I listen to them in conversation about the project it occurs to me that they are talking about some of the same ideals that I have championed many years ago.

In my life I have worn many hats. Personal hats and community hats. Today I realize that it may be time to put on a new hat. Perhaps the hat of elder; I am the oldest in the group after all. I must admit that some of my ideas are older, I don't think that they are antiquated, just different. For example, I use paper and pen to take notes, I like to make a chart to define how something is organized. Taking notes on a cell phone seems to me unwieldy as does communicating by text.

I have old hat ways of doing things and probably old hat ways of thinking about them. So, Betty, what to do? Will I choose to wear a new hat or will I be satisfied to put away my old hat and simply learn the new ways

of the youngers? A wise woman hat sounds appealing.
We will see!

Old Hats Have Character,

Me

How many old hats do you wear?

Which old hats are you willing to put away?

How do you feel about wearing a new hat?

Enough Already

August 5, 2024

Dear Betty,

Once again, I find myself thinking about the old aunties. What was it that seemed to give them the air of peace and patience? I do not recall ever seeing any one of them ranting or complaining or in today's language stressed out. Oh Betty, they did their fair share of complaining by way of their gossiping. Again, today we might say sharing over the peeling of potatoes or washing the dishes. But away from the kitchen, they were as composed as cool cucumbers.

What do I want from them today? I want to know why enough was enough for them. They seemed to me comfortable in their own skin, happy to be wives, mothers, at times volunteers and companions for one another. Was it enough? Maybe in their minds it was not ladylike to want more or to question the kinds of self-improvement that is so promoted today.

They were, I think, too busy doing their lives to worry about if they were enough. Without the bombardment of social media, T.V. and self-help gurus constantly banging on the doors of "be more", they were simply happy and wise in knowing just who they were and who they would continue to be, a world without end amen.

Enough,

Me

Do you think that you are enough?

What does a woman who you see as enough look like?

How can we acquire an air of peace and patience?

Perspective at 80

August 5, 2024

Dear Betty,

Many years ago I collaborated with an artist friend of mine to produce a coffee table book. It was her art and my writing. I met with her and my little tape recorder and had her tell me what each of the drawings meant to her. So Betty, here is the interesting part. She said that she just drew what interested her in terms of her print-making. Something happened though, as I listened to her talk about each piece, I could sense that there was deeper meaning in her work. We had different perspectives about them.

I wrote about each piece in her voice. I was experiencing a new way of listening. As I listened to her description of each piece, I felt her story evolving. She was as surprised as I was at what was being revealed.

My mom was never one to mince words. I gave her a copy of the book and she said that she would read it. The next week when I went to visit her, she told me that she had indeed read the book and that she thought that it was very spiritual. Not at all what I expected. And so, Betty, another perspective. Coming from my mom, it was a wow moment. She got it. In fact, she got more out of it than I did.

Betty, do our perspectives change with age? Will my grandchildren or great-grandchildren read these letters and wonder why I was so confused about perspectives? How will they form their own? I am convinced that the answer is yes. Another way to experience this crazy life journey, looking for new perspectives. What fun!

Thanks Mom,

Me

Have your perspectives changed as you travel the aging road?

What do you think about finding or looking for new perspectives?

How will you present new perspectives to others?

Envy

August 7, 2024

Dear Betty,

"Envy; We love in others what we lack ourselves, and would be everything but what we are."

- Richard Stoddard

Don't you think that we all have envy about something? If not at this minute but at some time in our lives, we must have noticed this uncomfortable feeling. Is envy different from jealousy?

Envy is "the painful feeling of wanting what someone else has," If you're jealous, you feel "threatened, protective, or fearful of losing to someone else." The other day I looked out of my window to see the girls working in the garden. They were picking the vegetables, weeding, and just making sure that everything was in order.

I wish I could be out there with them. Oh, yes, Betty I can physically walk out there and maybe even pick a few things but I for sure do not have the energy or stamina that they have. It was very hot and humid. They were bending, picking, and stretching to reach the plants. I remember those days and yes, I guess I am a bit envious. In that moment, I wanted to experience the same energy they have. I wanted to feel full of life. I am not jealous, because I do not feel threatened or fearful of losing anything. I already have, it is recognition of what it means to be eighty.

Perhaps I am now willing to say that I am resigned to my current reality. Will I feel envious of other things as time goes on? Yes, I suppose that I will, but for now I am grateful for their willingness to share their energy and their produce.

Just a little envious,

Me

What might you say that you are envious about now?

How does it make you feel when you recognize that you are envious?

What is it that you think you might want that could make you feel envy?

Tired

August 8, 2024

Dear Betty,

Being tired is getting really frustrating. I bet you are tired of hearing me tell you that I am tired as well. I think it is the single most telling issue when we are experiencing grief. Fatigue was not a word that I used to apply to myself until Don died. Then, Betty, there was no other way to describe what I was feeling, tired. When my fatigue dissipated, I felt relieved. Maybe there would be some days and then some more days that I would feel awake and aware, experiencing the fullness of life once again.

Today, Betty, I am once again longing for those days. Breathing in the fullness of life. Full of at least a modicum of energy and focus. Greeting the day with anticipation of what I will do, accomplish or ponder. I am drifting along, lost in the memories of my dear friends who have ended their journey here in my neighborhood. I miss them too much. Can I miss them too much? If they were here, I would be able to call them and they would tell me to stop whining. They would tell me to get on with it. They would tell me that they love me and that they know that this too shall end. But they are not just a phone call away. Thank my lucky stars that you are just a click away on my computer. You help me process and you help me have a reality check. You, Betty, move me on.

I hope that others find their Bettys!

Finding fullness in words,

Me

What do you find helpful when you need to process your journey?

How do you experience "fullness of life"? What does that mean to you?

Prayer

August 9, 2024

Dear Betty,

I have been trying to be very intentional about not turning my letters to you into a personal journal. So, I have purposefully not mentioned prayer or anything to do with my spiritual journey. How silly is that? How can I begin to understand life at eighty without recognizing all of the paths I have taken thus far? I need to awaken again to the spirit within.

The earliest time I can recall being devout was when I was eight and receiving my first Holy Communion. The Franciscan Sister who was my teacher was an amazing woman. She was kind, soft spoken, and loving. Generally, children are taught to bow their heads when it is time for the consecration but this nun told us not to do that. She said you look right at the host and you say, "my Lord and my God" because Jesus loves you. I have been unchurched now for some time but I always remember that nun, her gentle eyes and her wise words. Prayer was also an important part of my family life. No, Betty, we didn't pray together at home but we never missed Sunday Mass. My mother was an avid candle lighter. We lit candles for the living and for the dead. We participated in the rituals of death and dying and she made sure that we all received the sacraments.

Recently, well maybe over the past several years I have thought about going "back" to church. I think I have found the right church home for myself. It is a small church with a community that is made up of people that dare I say, appear to be my peer group. This little church is old and unassuming, just like me. Prayers are offered and bread is broken. Fellowship follows. I am beginning to feel my spiritual juices returning. Candles are still lit in my home and in my children's homes. We pray for many intentions. I prayed when Don was dying. I prayed for patience and I prayed that he could sleep in peace.

Hands folded,

Me

Who are your spiritual role models or guides?

How do you experience prayer?

What rituals do you still hold to and share with others?

The Waters Fine

August 10, 2024

Dear Betty,

Many years ago, I was visiting my dear friend. We were sitting on the pier looking over the lake. It was a really hot and humid summer day. I suggested something completely out of character for me: I said that we should jump into the lake to cool off. Yes, Betty, in our clothes. With a little whining and convincing she finally agreed. We joined hands and jumped into the water.

Although I didn't know it then, it was one of those moments in your life when something changed inside. I grew up a good girl, obeyed the rules, followed the prescribed path. But, there I was, a grown woman with almost grown children of my own, taking a leap into what would become a life of challenges, service, and amazing adventures.

How strange it is Betty that I should be relating this story to you now as I try to navigate my eighties. Once again, I am not so sure that I am willing to trust my instincts and jump off of any pier. Should I stay on dry land, safe, and familiar? New challenges are beginning to surface and I wonder if I will take the plunge.

I hear you Betty, telling me, "Come on, jump in, the water's fine."

Off the pier,

Me

Have you ever had a moment when you just knew something in you changed? Explain.

How willing are you to trust your instincts?

Backsliding

August 11, 2024

Dear Betty,

The garden is planted and growing. It is too late to decide that it is too large or that it is too difficult to take care of. The garden has a mind of its own and growing it will. I could pull out the plants but that would be sad because I would not have the benefit of using the fruits of the effort that was put into the creation. Growing is a difficult process requiring watering and weeding out what might stop the process.

Lately Betty, I have been thinking about backsliding. For some months now I have been working hard on planting and growing my inner garden. Sorting or weeding out what has been useful and what has not. It is hard work, this inner gardening. Can I decide to go back to the long days of feeling lost, alone and with no direction or purpose? This would be serious backsliding. I am not one to give up on anything that easily. Maybe like the aunties, I have some grit after all. Yes Betty, there are days when I want to accept the stereotype image of the eighty-year-old-white-haired woman walking with a cane going nowhere special.

But like the garden that continues to grow despite the weeds and lacking water, I refuse to go back, to discount all of the hard work that I have done and I refuse to discount the learnings as well. My inner garden may

not be picture perfect but it is me and today it is filled
with roses and lilies.

Growing and living,

Me

*How do you feel about planting your own inner
garden?*

Does this metaphor work for you?

*What do you do when you feel yourself backsliding in
negativity?*

Urgency

August 14, 2024

Dear Betty,

One of the things that I believe I have learned about this exploration of aging at eighty is a silent request deep inside of myself for urgency. There are soft summer days when I sit on the porch, grateful for the gentle breeze rustling the branches of the huge evergreen trees. The very trees that we planted when they were small and seemed to beg for nurturing. There is no urgency then. I am quiet and at peace.

At other times the silent request inside urges me to get moving, do something, find a way, join a group, don't go back to sleep. It is a conundrum. Betty, I have made a decision to do something that I would never have thought I would do. I spent time in conversation with others, I prayed, I discerned and then I took the leap and said yes, I will do it. Of course, in the way of the world, the next stage of the process is, "wait for all of the puzzle pieces to fall into place." But I say to you, Betty, I don't have a whole life ahead of me anymore. I have to make good use of my time; I don't appreciate waiting much anymore.

You see how silly this sounds? Or maybe not. Maybe I just have to accept that there are times to be quiet and at peace, resting in holy breezes, and then there are times for get up and go, get it done. Two sides of the same coin make it worth something, don't you think?

Urgently waiting,

Me

How often do you feel an urgency in your life?

Do you find yourself feeling the sense of urgency in deeper ways as you age?

Do you think that urgency and "get up and go" are two sides of the same coin?

Picture Perfect

August 15, 2024

Dear Betty,

For many years I put on the mantle of perfectionism. Now at eighty I have thrown off the mantle and replaced it with a jaunty hat.

Today the small group of women that I gather with each month will be arriving at my home. Since I no longer wear the mantle of perfectionism, I even have a moment to write to you Betty.

I am ready to greet them, the cake is made, the coffee warm and the cups lay ready to be filled. The cushions on the chairs have been fluffed. I am ready. Why is it that we spend so many days of our lives worrying about making sure that everything is perfect? Of course, you know why Betty, it is because we use it as a measure of our level of personhood. If all that we do and all that we think and all those others think about us is perfect, then we survive our moments of low or nonexistent self-esteem. It is a goal that is not achievable.

All women, I fear, have the need to feel perfect even if we don't use those words. We want to be recognized as having a worthy word to share, we want to present ourselves as "having it all together." Why? There is not one thing in nature that is totally and completely perfect. How boring it would be if that were not true. A little quirkiness and an attitude of acceptance for being just who I am, authentic and true, seems to me to be a happier and wholly better way to perceive myself, my life and the world around me. Only you are perfect Betty, praise be to God.

Imperfect picture,

Me

How do you feel about making sure that all is perfect?

What if there is a little dust on the coffee table or the coffee is still perking?

What do you need to have an attitude of acceptance about?

Days of Glory

August 18, 2024

Dear Betty

Today began with a note of sadness. I looked out of my bedroom window and noticed that my flowers that are sitting nicely in pots on the front porch were looking less than perky. The hanging basket was not looking well either. I quickly took to getting them a large drink of water. I am not sure that it will be enough, but I am just not ready for this to be happening. It is just too early.

Then I went to church. Last Sunday, the gardens outside of the little church were amazingly beautiful. Today they too were looking sad. The daylilies were actually drooping with their leaves turning brown.

What does this mean? Are we going to have an early fall? Who knows? On the other hand, I am now thinking that it is another way of nature telling me what to expect during this leg of the long journey. At a time not so long ago, I felt pretty perky, ambitious almost. These days, like my porch flowers, I have days of glory. Other days I have days of waning. It is true I just do not have the same long-term growing power. Here is that quote again. "I went fast all of my life, now I am going slow" –Maria Shriver. Slow doesn't mean stopped, just taking a breath.

Waning a little,

Me

How do you celebrate your days of glory?

What do you think about the quote from Maria Shriver?

What do you see in nature that explains your personal aging journey?

Calendar Pages

August 19, 2024

Dear Betty,

The end of summer signals the arrival of fall. Fall is the season of harvesting, getting ready for winter, taking advantage of the last lovely days and the most beautiful colors that the trees can produce.

Today I realize that if I would use the seasons as metaphor for these eighties then, something is amiss. I was writing something on my calendar and I noticed that there were several squares with writing on them. I bet you are thinking, "so what?" Well, for the last several months the squares have been mostly empty. I feel like something has shifted. Maybe I am harvesting after all. Gathering the fruit of my waiting labors.

Betty, I do seem to be more conscious of things happening around me. I am noticing little signs and wonders and have even had some of them pointed out to me by others. I don't want to sound over the top metaphysically but there is a different kind of energy in me. I am both willing to leave the noise and haste of the world behind me and I am willing to move with the questions being asked.

If this is the rhythm of life in the eighties, then so far it has been challenging. It is also interesting, frustrating and happy. I will gratefully wait for the beautiful contrasting colors and the warm sweaters of fall.

Turning calendar pages,

Me

What are you harvesting, gathering into yourself, for the journey ahead?

How does your energy change with the seasons?

Scary New Adventures

August 20, 2024

Dear Betty,

This new adventure is really scary. I don't know anything about getting our letters published. I realize that I haven't felt scared for some time. I wasn't even scared when Don was sick and when he died. I had so many other emotions then but "scared" was not one of them.

So, Betty, what is so scary now? Maybe you can help me unpack my current feelings. Yes? I thought that what I was feeling was the fear of being disappointed. Trust has never been an issue for me. In fact, I usually jump in with both feet to share, or listen, or provide help. I realize now that this is not always the best way to be. Disappointment is not foreign to me and yet I find that when visited by it, I respond differently now than I did in my earlier decades. Were those times about disappointment or were they deeper feelings of not being enough or understood or listened too? Perhaps all of that but maybe simply living a different reality than those involved.

If I am facing fear, what am I afraid of? Well, Betty, it is the same old thing. Acceptance. Will others appreciate my work? Will I receive understanding? Am I wasting my time? All of these are rhetorical questions. I need to get over myself and listen to all of the kind and supportive words that I have received, remembering that I am appreciated and loved.

Unpacked,

Me

What might the feelings be for you when you have experienced disappointment?

How do you process your feelings of fear or of not being understood?

Do you have someone in your life that can help you unpack feelings? Is it a mutual sharing relationship?

Day Off

August 21, 2024

Dear Betty,

It has been a really busy week. Lots of things to do and lots of things to think about. I thought that I would just take the day off. I am at home. Sometimes it is so lovely to just be at home. And sometimes not so much.

I received a call today from my cousin. We are planning a get together of all of the cousins. The conversation, of course, didn't stop at just talking about the event to come. It never does. It was a good talk, but one that required thinking.

In just a few days I am officiating a memorial service. It is a little complicated and at times they are. I am working hard and thinking about ways to make it meaningful for two sides of bereaved family and friends that don't always agree. I know that all will be well. It just takes a lot of thought.

The manuscript collection of our Letters Betty was sent off to the publisher yesterday. Now I am trying not to think about what her answer will be. I am trying hard not to think about all of the things that she may not like. I am trying hard to be positive. Afterall, Betty, our letters have been and continue to be part of my healing journey and so far, they are doing their job.

Aside from all of that thinking that I really don't want to do today, I awoke promising myself a day off. What a silly goose I am. Maybe tomorrow.

To think or not to think,

Me

Do you know when you need to take a day off and if you do, how do you feel afterwards?

What is it that you need to take some time to think about?

Control What?

August 23, 2024

Dear Betty.

I have been invited to a couple of events that I think would be really fun. However, I am realizing that my age is interfering with my immediately saying yes! It is all about control. Not the kind that I have spent a good share of my life trying to be smart about, no, this kind of control has more to do with age issues.

Do you think that I have gotten too comfortable with being at home or only doing the things that give me control? I mean, if I say yes to these events I start thinking about things like: how far do I have to walk? Will there be bathrooms available? What about food? Will there be options for us older folks?

I have not decided as yet if I will swim out into the deep water of still another challenge to my independence or will I buckle down to my insecurities and stay home wishing that I would have said yes.

Undecided,

Me

Do you think that age, or being older, has much to do with your willingness to say yes to new challenges?

What do you think you need to control to be authentic in your aging journey?

Going Slow or Not

August 24, 2024

Dear Betty,

Do you remember what I said lately about going slow? Me neither. Today I do not feel like I am slow. I have made a really big decision. I am going to have *Letters to Betty: The Anatomy of One Woman's Grief* published. This is the last thing that I thought I would be doing now at eighty.

I have seen many stories about women, olders like me, who have continued to do amazing, helpful and challenging things. Never did I ever think that I would be pursuing, sharing my thoughts, feelings and words in this way.

For so many months I wondered what I might do next. What were these years going to be like? The calendar was pretty empty. Today it seems to be filling up and I am feeling like I am once again going fast. I need to remind myself, slow is good. Sometimes slow is very very good.

Kinda fast today, maybe slow tomorrow,

Me

Are you going fast or slow? Why is that?

Are you surprised by things that you are doing now that you didn't think you would ever be doing? Explain please!

Is That All There Is?

August 25, 2024

Dear Betty,

Peggy Lee sang the song "Is That All There Is?" I always thought that it was such a sad song. It didn't seem to have any hope. It was all about the sad story of a person, who I thought had so many difficult things happen in their life that they wondered if that was all. Where was the more?

Betty, I will confess that I have had those kinds of days. Don't we all wonder at times why there isn't more: more to our lives, more to our loves, more to our days?

Today I went to my new church. The people there are so welcoming. It is such a tiny church that sometimes there are no more than 10 people there praying. But I feel the sincerity of their prayer and their invitation to be one of them. Each time I attend they invite me to join them afterward for coffee. Today they even asked me to stay even though they were having a meeting. Wow, Betty, they are just so open. They make me feel like there is more and I can be a part of it. When I am there, I don't feel like I think that there should be more. It is enough.

I finally decided to look at all of the lyrics. The chorus suits me. It is of course open to interpretation but today and maybe, I hope, that for some days to come I will enjoy remembering, to keep dancing, to break out the booze, and have a ball. Not literally of course.

Dancing and having a ball,

Me

Do you feel like there should be more to your life than you are experiencing today?

What more would you like, how do you answer the question, "Is that all there is?"

Just Thank You Will do

August 26, 2024

Dear Betty,

Today I am wondering why it is so hard to accept a simple compliment. When we were children, we were taught to say thank you when someone gave us one. "What a cute dress."

"Just say thank you," said Mom.

Yesterday I attended church. Afterward a woman who I have seen there a few times said, "I like your dress, you always wear dresses that are so colorful," Did I just say thank you Betty? No. I proceeded to justify why I wear colorful dresses.

"I like color," I said.

As children we are just happy that someone noticed us and said something nice. As an older I was dismayed with myself for still being uncomfortable with a compliment. I suppose if we take this to the nth degree, we could discover that even at eighty self-doubt creeps in, self-image is top of mind. Betty, I thought that I was past all of that stuff. Guess not.

I am going to try to be more childlike about some things, one of them being, just saying thank you.

Thank you,

Me

What do you think about just saying thank you?

What makes us think that we have to respond to a compliment with more than a simple thanks?

Sweet Tomorrow

August 27, 2024

Dear Betty,

Not too long ago, just a few months actually, I found myself watching the clock until it was time for bed. Days seemed long and I wanted the comfort of soft bed and cozy covers. It became my cocoon, my safe place. It was as though I was thinking that I had made it through another purposeless day. Was this going to be my new reality?

Remember me writing about the blank calendar Betty? Well, it isn't blank any longer. I feel as though I am engaging again. I have met interesting people at the little church that I like very much. I found a ministry officiating memorial services, and I was asked to take care of my great-grandson. Friends have invited me to lunch.

Last night I found that I was not very interested in the selections on the T.V. even though it has tons of choices. I was thinking about the day past and I found myself anxious for bedtime. What was different, Betty? I was looking forward to tomorrow. I was anxious, the good kind, to get to bed because tomorrow promised to be sweet.

I hope that your tomorrows are also sweet and longed for Betty.

Here comes tomorrow,

Me

How do you feel about your "tomorrows"?

What do you think you might feel if your calendar was empty?

How important is it for elders to feel purposeful?

What would a "sweet tomorrow" look like for you?

A Little Joy

August 28, 2024

Dear Betty,

I just wrote a letter on my very nice stationary. It has a matching envelope and even a sticker on the back. It made me feel good. I remembered when we learned how to write a proper letter, write out the address and seal it. I remember too how good it felt to take it to the post office and send it off to someone special. What was even more exciting was getting a letter back.

It makes me a little sad that the joy of this kind of communication has been lost on my children and grandchildren. It is the feeling of reaching out to someone and sharing something with them in a very special and personal way. Then there is the anticipation of waiting for an answer. It is not the same as sealing a bill and sending it off hoping that it will get to where you want it to go.

So today I am feeling joy and happiness in just one of life's little pleasures.

Hoping it arrives,

Me

What are the little things in life that bring you joy?

How do you think about creating joy by reaching out to someone else?

What are the ways that you communicate these days?

Living Wholistically

August 29, 2024

Dear Betty,

Body, mind, and emotions. Emotions get ignored beyond the expected feelings; the surface ones that aging brings. I was watching a tribute show about a country singer. The songs that were being used as a eulogy were many of the songs that reminded me of Don. He was a fan of country music and sang many of their songs. I was having a particularly weepy day. I don't know why Betty, that hasn't happened to me for some time now. I think it was the memory of hearing the songs at another time in my life.

Why do we get more emotional about these kinds of things as we age? I don't know but I do know that I am more susceptible to what some folks might call sappy. I have also noticed that older men seem to tear up and I don't recall them being free with their tears when they were younger.

Emotions seem to be closer to the forefront for those of us at or nearing the eighties. They take over, have their way with us. Memories seem to catapult to the surface forcing us to pay attention, nagging us and not to be ignored.

Living holistically then, I guess, means that I have just one more thing to pay attention to for all of the years of eighty to come.

Emotionally speaking,

Me

Do you feel that your emotions are closer to the forefront now?

What do you do when your emotions make a surprise visit?

How do you feel about the memories that come to the surface when you least expect them?

A Big and Empty House

August 30, 2024

Dear Betty,

It was a gloomy day. I looked around and realized that I live in a rather large house. Lately I find myself thinking that not only is my house big, (really only by my standard) but empty. What is empty about it, you might ask, Betty? It is missing many of the things that were ours together. Things that we collected on our travels, things that were given to us through the years and especially the sounds of a family living a happy, busy life.

There are still plenty of "things" in the big house. They just don't have the same value or meaning that the ones that are missing held. There are treasures that are only mine. Gifts from dear friends, things that hold special memories. Simple things, favorite books, music, and my favorite quilt.

Funny Betty, the things that cross my mind now. At eighty I seem to be more introspective. I guess that is one of the things that I hear is usual about becoming an older. Are there things that are usual at this age? What will happen during the rest of the years of eighty? I bet that you thought that I was going to say that I am lonely in my big and empty house. Not today, but sometimes.

Waiting to find out,

Me

What are the things that you might miss if you were to do a clear out?

How do you find yourself feeling about becoming introspective?

What is usual for you at this stage of life?

Toss and Turn

August 31, 2024

Dear Betty,

Having spent many nights tossing and turning it occurred to me this morning that it just might be a good or maybe great metaphor for my search for meaning at eighty.

For the past couple of decades, I have done my share of tossing and turning. Rolling from one side of the bed to the other, trying to find a comfortable spot, and then after just a few minutes deciding that I was not comfortable at all.

Trying to figure out life at eighty finds me tossing and turning. I just about think that I have found some comfort and acceptance when I start turning again to doubt and, if I am honest, fear. This tossing and turning means that the process starts all over again. Guilty, frustrated, and embarrassed are only a few of the emotions that come along with tossing and turning, if one sleeps with a partner. Not so different when used as a metaphor.

However, the process in and of itself could easily be identified in those of us who find ourselves sleeping alone. Now, Betty, how is this a metaphor for getting older? Let me start with tossing. As I think about what I am going to do each day or week or maybe even the rest of this eightieth year, there are things that I have tossed out. I toss out more freely now things that do not interest me, I try to toss out thoughts about things that I am fearful of or that plain and simply just piss me off. In my sorting, I find myself not just tossing but turning as well. I am turning to more time to think things through. I am turning to asking for sound counsel. I find myself turning to you, Betty, to help me identify my feelings when I start tossing.

Just as I used to feel guilty or frustrated or embarrassed about my bed etiquette, I feel guilty at times for not trying harder. I am frustrated that seven months have gone by and I am not so sure that I have answered any of my own questions about this year. I am embarrassed when someone asks me "how are you?" and I still don't have a really good answer.

I guess, Betty, that I just need to be willing to be, turn to quiet porch time, and kind counsel. It is the best kind of turning and saves me from too much tossing.

Being still,

Me

Do you think tossing and turning is a good metaphor for your own journey?

What might you be willing to toss out and what do you want to hold on to a bit longer?

What will you turn to that might help you find answers when you need them?

September

Labor

September 1, 2024

Dear Betty,

"To labor - to strive to effect or achieve. To exert one's powers of body or mind especially with painful or strenuous effort." – Merriam–Webster Dictionary

This being Labor Day I thought it might be wise to think about what that word means to me today. Yes, we retire from our jobs, our work and to some extent what we would describe as our labor, being in the labor force. But, Betty, I said to myself, "How or what am I laboring about today?"

Referring back to the definition, I might say that I am striving to affect a modicum of understanding about my life today. What am I hoping to achieve? How much of my body or mind am I willing to give to this effort?

Now I come back to the word itself, labor. When a woman is in labor, she is striving to have a baby. I would like to jump onto this metaphor and say that she is hoping and praying to achieve new life. That is the idea that I want to stay with today. If I am striving and putting strenuous effort into understanding, to awareness of who I am and what I do now, my hope and prayer is that it produces new life as well.

Well, Betty I think that our work might, to use an old phrase, be a labor of love and so then we will work at it with strenuous effort. When the time comes to labor no more, we will say, we gave it our all.

Willing to labor,

Me

What are you laboring over or about today?

How much strenuous effort are you willing to give to your aging journey?

What would you consider "NEW LIFE" that you are willing to labor for?

Reality Check

September 2, 2024

Dear Betty,

Yesterday was the memorial for a friend. I officiated the Celebration of Life. He was eighty-eight years old and so many of those attending the memorial were, I surmise, well over sixty-five. As I looked over the gathering it was evident that his grandchildren looked and felt out of place. Betty, it seems to me that I am often the one I feel looks out of place.

Being with these wonderful, caring olders was certainly a reality check for me. Why is it that I just don't see myself in them? I am probably older than most of them. I just don't feel it inside my inner being. How do I know that though? I can't know how they feel about this part of life's journey. I am just making judgments that I fear are out of line.

Still, Betty, it's a reality check. I cannot deny that I am eighty, no, part eighty now. I am learning and growing and experiencing so many things on this journey to the eighty-ones, eighty-twos, eighty-threes, etc.

Holding at eighty till then,

Me

When do you feel out of place, or do you ever?

Do you see yourself in other elders and how do you feel about that?

How do you feel about receiving these reality checks from time to time?

Perspective

September 3, 2024

Dear Betty,

Looking out of my office window this morning, I noticed that if I focus on trying to see all the way to the tree line at the end of the eighty acres of course the trees and fields closest to me are large. The trees and fields across the acres grow smaller and smaller.

This study in perspective is so interesting. It speaks to me of my journey. The things closest to my mind and heart seem so big and maybe at times unsurmountable. If I stretch my view, if I change my focus, I realize that it may be a long journey to the back forty or the end of the eighty acres but I can see and the end is in sight.

As I journey through this year of eighty and beyond, I must say that I am enjoying the lessons that I am gleaning from nature. A simple look out of my window graced me with yet another insight. Eighty is good!

Well, Betty, I am off to do my ordinary things for today. I wonder what lessons there are in the discomfort caused by ragweed and other pollens at this time of the year? HUM...another day.

Busy mind today,

Me

Do you find lessons in nature? How do you react to them?

Can you think of a metaphor that describes your perspective as an elder?

Should we even think about our perspective as part of our aging journey?

The Widow

September 4, 2024

Dear Betty,

This week is the anniversary of Don's death. I was so confident that I was just going to go through it like any other week. Silly me. The memories of those last few days with him keep running through my mind like an old slideshow, a little dull, no sound, haunting me with the same old questions that I had so surely put behind me. At least I thought that I had put them behind me. I do not feel any guilt about what I might have done or should have done or what someone else might have done. I am at peace with our last few days together.

Do I have wishes, Betty? You bet I do. I selfishly wish that we would have had more time. Yes, I know that this is a selfish wish. Still, I miss him. I miss his voice, his proclaiming that he was home, his phone calls telling me that he was on his way. His, "I love you."

This widow business has also been on my mind. Do you remember Betty, the old movies and T.V. shows when they would refer to some of the women as "the widow so and so?" I really don't want to be introduced as the Widow Bub. I guess I have spent too much of my life finding my voice in all of its characters or roles. I really like my current moniker, Nana. I was remembering how others introduced us to others. I don't think anyone ever said Mr. and Mrs. Usually Don and Mary, and when the grandkids started to come, we became Nana and Papa. I remember a time when our oldest was in middle school and one day she announced that she was not going to call me mama or mom any more. She decided to call me mother. That didn't last long. It is so interesting how the small parts of our lives that we just don't pay much attention to unless an event like this week of first anniversary tosses us into our reverie.

The Widow Bub,

Me

What are the images you might see if you thought of your life as a slideshow?

How many ways have you been identified?

What are some of the small parts of your life that you want to pay attention to?

Sailing

September 6, 2024

Dear Betty,

Yesterday I went on a trip to Moline, Illinois. With my daughter and son-in-law. We took a bus to East Moline and then did a day cruise on the Celebration Belle. It is a replica of an old paddleboat on the Mississippi.

It was a lovely early fall day, cool in the morning and really warm in the afternoon. We met many other people, some older and some younger and some the same era as us. I still find it interesting Betty, the way I feel about being with groups like this. I know that they are my peers and still I don't feel like I totally belong. This is really a complicated feeling for me because I might guess that I am probably one of the olders.

All in all, it was a good day. It was also nice to spend some time away with the kids who are themselves roaring past middle age and almost to retirement. Maybe what I don't like about doing these kinds of things is the reality that hits me square in the face. I am one of them and maybe I should act like them, do the things that they do, and get over myself. Betty, I just don't think so.

Suffice it to say that I did enjoy the day, the boat trip down the Mississippi, the entertainment and, yes, the company.

Down the river,

Me

How do you feel about being with your peer group?

Where do you most feel like you belong?

What is the most important thing on your bucket list if you have one?

Tottering

September 7, 2024

Dear Betty,

Since yesterday was the first anniversary of Don's death, today I am wondering if I count today as the first day of my new year at eighty or will that start with my birthday? Perhaps today will be remembered as the first day of another year without him.

I am happy that I decided to publish our letters about my grief process. You helped me through that and now here I am still writing about moments of lingering grief. What did I think, Betty? Did I really think that I would simply move on to focusing on our new letters? Once again, I am writing, silly me.

Wherever our letters take me, I hope to be open to the process. I hope to be of some service to another soul who like me needs help on this last leg of life's journey.

Tottering on,

Me

What does tottering mean to you?

How many times will you just want to totter on?

How open are you to whatever new process you are facing?

Absent-Minded

September 8, 2024

Dear Betty,

You will not believe what I did today. I put York outside. Then I left and when I came back, I didn't find him anywhere. I had left him tied outside. Don't worry Betty, he was not out for too long. What is this about I thought? I have never done this before.

Too many things swirling around in my mind, I think. I wonder if this is another symptom of the eighties? I haven't noticed that I have been particularly absent-minded about anything else. No, Betty, I think I still have my facilities and do not find myself getting lost at the end of my driveway. Paying more attention, staying focused, and not wandering off into too many alleys in my mind may keep me from doing this again. One can hope.

A long time ago there was a movie or maybe a T.V. show and in it one of the characters, said, "It was in the far reaches of my absent mind." We used to say that often when a strange fact or memory would surface. Where did that come from? The far reaches of my absent mind. A fun way to explain having an interesting thought. It is far different than being absent-minded.

I think I will try not to lose myself in my far reaches and hope that I will not become ever more absent-minded as I continue this eighties journey.

Fully in tact today,

Me

How many times do you think that you are absent-minded when in fact you are just stressed and have too many things on your mind?

How do you feel about exploring the far reaches of your absent mind?

Are you concerned about becoming absent-minded?

Faith vs. Works

September 9, 2024

Dear Betty,

Yesterday I heard a sermon asking the question, "What good is it if you say that you have faith but you do not have 'works'?" This one question amidst all of the rest that somehow has stayed with me. I believe that I have faith.

I have faith in the values that I was taught as a child. I have faith in my children and grandchildren and along with faith I have hope. I hope that they will continue to follow the path that has gotten them to where they are today.

What about me? How has my faith changed at this time of my life?

Perhaps it is stronger in my beliefs of some things and not so much in others. But, Betty, what are my works? What are the works of anyone who has begun the final journey?

Since I have been writing to you and sharing some of our letters with trusted friends I have been affirmed. They have shared with me gifts and talents that they think I have that I have not really accepted for myself like being an artist or a writer. Now I am beginning to have faith in their assessment of me. Now I am beginning to have faith or to believe that these things, doing art or writing, might be my works.

Betty, it is what I choose to do with them that will stand the test of faith. If I continue to share my work and my words in the service of others, then I can hold on to the fact that my faith is not dead. The lessons learned all of these years have not been for naught.

Faithfully,

Me

How would you describe yourself as a person of faith?

What are the lessons learned long ago that still give you peace and hope?

What has changed in how you feel about faith as you age?

Hurrying

September 10, 2024

Dear Betty,

I am trying, working at doing my best to go slow. It is a hard goal to achieve. The world around me, my environment, continues to call me to keep moving, doing, being.

It is also difficult to go slow when others around me are going very, very fast. Some of them are working, "familying", socializing and so they have many things on their plates. At times I grow weary of the speed of my life. I wait for a visit and then it comes and then it is over all too soon. Betty, I confess that I wish the visits were not so often interrupted by the hurriedness of others.

There are days in which I am not hurrying at all. I am taking time to enjoy my coffee, perhaps a phone conversation with a friend. Writing to you. But, the little voice in my head starts to butt in and reminds me that my days are numbered. There are far too few of them to be sitting around going slow. I find myself inventing things to do that I might hurry through.

Trying not to hurry, but Betty, maybe I should. Would it make my days seem more meaningful if I was more engaged in a multitude of things? Why do I not think that enjoying my coffee and spending time in quietude is not meaningful or important for a woman at eighty?

Just a moment,

Me

What do you think about the idea of going slow?

Do you think hurrying is a good way to cope with aging?

Is it stressful for you to go slow, take time in quietude?

A New Kind of Fear

September 11, 2024

Dear Betty,

You and I have traveled down this road many times. Listing so many things that brought fear to our door. As a young woman wondering and fearing what adulthood would hold for me. As a young wife, I hoped that I would measure up when attending my first grown-up Christmas party with my husband at his place of work. As a mother, well, Betty, you know what kind of fear that can bring. Far too many to account for here. Retirement and midlife hold its own doubt and anxiety. Mostly I find that this time of life brings with it identity crises. Who will I be now since all of the roles that I have played are no longer part of my everyday life?

One by one all the fears of a life are either faced or buried. Unfortunately, some of them surface when we least expect them and we have to make the choice again and again. Betty, you have helped me become rather fearless in most things.

I find myself now facing a new kind of fear. I don't even know how to name it or explain. I can tell you that it is a scary feeling and it makes my heart shutter. Mostly I find it knocking on my door when I try to be a good citizen and listen to all of the political nonsense of the current election. I have throughout my life at all of its ages and stages tried to be aware of the social aspects that affect my family and my community. I have never been afraid of what might be the result of an election. I am frightened now.

At eighty this current season of discontent in our politics is not only challenging me with a new kind of fear, it is also making me feel helpless. I, outside of my own family and circle of friends, don't really know what I can do to be the change that I want to happen. Betty, I am offended by the casual way name calling and lying is accepted. Today, I have no answers and I am not sure that I have any questions that make sense either.

Shedding off unwanted fear,

Me

Do you have unwanted fears? Can you name them?

What are some fears that you have now that you didn't have before?

Can't – Can

September 13, 2024

Dear Betty,

Yesterday would have been my friend Susan's birthday. When these anniversaries appear, they make me wonder just what it is that I am supposed to do. I can't be with her, well not physically anyway. I can remember all of the past birthdays that we have shared together. So happy birthday Susan.

I have also been thinking about all of the things that I cannot do anymore. I do not climb ladders; I have difficulty with some housekeeping tasks. This kind of thinking tends to make me feel maudlin. I prefer to focus on the things that I can do. I am living independently; I can still drive and get to where I want to go. There is quite a list of my I cans.

This reflection has also led me to think about not only what I can't do but also what I won't do. I refuse to compromise those things that I hold dear. I hope to keep close to my values. I will accept help when I need it but it makes me a little cranky when told that I shouldn't be doing some things because I am after all old.

I think that this is a study that could go on for some time. Maybe a good topic for a discussion. But for now, I think I will go and take a nap.

Because I can,

Me

What are you doing that you still can and what are you not doing?

How difficult is it to accept the fact that there are things that you can and cannot do?

Clearly

September 15, 2024

Dear Betty,

While trying to decide what I was feeling today, I kept coming back to the word clear. I notice that for the last several years I have used the word clearly a lot. It seems to say, absolutely, no question. Then at other times I use it as a way to say, well of course that's the case, what else could it be?

I find that I get more and more frustrated when in a gathering or a meeting that has a clear agenda and the conversation is not clear. Sometimes I think that it is just convoluted and made more complicated than it needs to be.

This is another road marker on the road in my eighties. I find that I see things more clearly than I have before. Or maybe it is just that I am not as prone to engaging in silliness or conversation that is not productive. Now, Betty, I hear you asking, "can't conversation just be enjoyable or fun?" Well, of course it can, but for me it makes me much more comfortable when it comes to a point in a relatively short amount of time.

When I see things clearly, I can understand them. Clearly is also a great word to use when something's obvious. I confess Betty, I do not always monitor the tone of my voice when I say "clearly", meaning of course, or why don't you get it.

I love a clear day. I also love a relationship or conversation that is clear, meaning transparent. No dancing around trying to say or be or do something that is not authentic. Remember the song, "I can see clearly now" by Johnny Nash?

Today I can see clearly now. I recognize many of the obstacles that keep me from facing my eighties openly, authentically. Many of the dark clouds are gone, returning only briefly to remind me that I have clearly entered eighty.

Feeling Clear,

Me

What do you think that you see more clearly now than ever before?

What areas of your life are still hidden in dark clouds of fear or anxiety?

In Bed

September 16, 2024

Dear Betty,

Did you ever feel like you just wanted to stay in bed? I don't mean to infer that I am sad or depressed. Well not any more than usual anyway. I woke up this morning and just didn't want to leave my warm, comfortable bed.

Thinking about it today I wondered why I felt this way. At night when I go to bed, I often get settled and then take a long *awwwww* breath. It feels so good to let myself relax and sink into the comfort of my cocoon. I feel safe there but I at times also miss his presence. There is something about sharing a bed with another person, or a child or even a dog or cat or two. Just hearing the soft slow breathing of another gives peace.

Still Betty, I am beginning to think that the reason I like to stretch out, pull up the covers and stay in bed for just a little while longer, is because I know when I get up, I will be asking myself, what has to happen today? What are the ordinary things that I need to do? What surprises will there be? You would think that these questions alone would motivate me to get up sooner. Sometimes it is in those last few moments in bed that a really good idea comes to me or a really interesting phrase that I have been contemplating. Honestly there are times when I just don't want to face another day's challenges at eighty. Then I throw back the covers, put my feet on the floor, say good morning to my faithful dog, and get on with it.

I will tell you Betty; I do enjoy that first cup of coffee in the morning and of course I wouldn't be able to do that if I stayed in bed.

Awake now,

Me

How often do you just want to stay in bed?

What great ideas have you enjoyed just before you got out of bed?

Self-Talk and Talking to Myself

September 18, 2024

Dear Betty,

I laughed out loud the other day. I was in the kitchen frying some eggs. Then I heard myself talking out loud to no one but me. I laughed and then smiled. This seems to have become a regular thing with me. I don't recall talking out loud to myself in the past. I have had loud thoughts, but rarely spoke them.

This got me thinking about the difference between talking to myself and self-talk. The difference, as I see it, is that talking to myself seems spontaneous and has to do with whatever I am doing at the time. While self-talk is a practice that has come into vogue over the last few decades. In my work I have encouraged women to practice self-talk as a way to get in touch with their feelings. It is also a way to process thoughts and can help in making decisions. Usually, it is thought to be a good thing. Of course, there is the possibility that it can also be detrimental to someone who is suffering from depression or other mental anguish.

Well Betty, enough of that. I am thankful that I have been able to use self-talk as a way to remind myself that I am here, I am fine, I am good, and I am blessed. I can also find myself at times telling myself that I blew it, should have been better, who do I think I am? Since I have had the good grace to use positive self-talk it wins out.

Do you think that my talking to myself out loud will continue to make me laugh? Do you think that it will take the place of self-talk? Probably not, but it is an interesting problem to process today. Maybe it is another badge to add to my eldering banner, like a girl scout.

Quiet on all fronts now,

Me

What happens when you find yourself engaging in self-talk?

Does talking out loud to yourself help you process your feelings?

Feelings – Unnamed – Unrecognized

September 20, 2024

Dear Betty,

Do you think that we focus more on our feelings as we age or do you think that we just don't want to think about them any longer?

Sitting on the porch this morning, listening to the birds in the bird apartments and enjoying the early morning haze on the fields, I tried to name what I was feeling. It was the same feeling that I am wrapped in each and every day. What could I name it? I tried to find another word for sad but none came to my rescue. Sad just does not cover it. It is so many things. I, on any given day feel happy, concerned, creative, lonely, tired, or maybe weary. Now I think that all of my feelings land in a bushel basket, and this nameless feeling is the weaving that holds all of the others together in the basket. It is a little worn and sometimes a little frayed but somehow it is also being at home. It is where I live now. It is the place that I know, have known love, acceptance, and the meaning of relationship.

It is really hard Betty, to describe this feeling but I think that I will just keep trying. Why? I don't know, perhaps to reach some kind of understanding. I am sure that I am much more comfortable with this unnamed feeling than I am wondering how I feel about the unrecognized ones. I am actually proud of myself for my willingness to be aware of my feelings, whether I can identify them or not. We all know, Betty, the result of not facing the feelings that we just don't want to acknowledge. They don't go away as we age, they just cause more complications.

In the place I live,

Me

How do you feel about naming your feelings?

What is the consequence of living with unrecognized feelings?

How do you describe lingering sadness after a loss?

Intimacy

September 21, 2024

Dear Betty,

Thinking about intimacy at this stage of life somehow seems daunting to me. Still sitting on the porch this morning, I began to give it a whirl. Why is it, Betty, that we don't seem to be able to talk about intimacy without talking about sex? Sex is good, but for most of us olders it is a long past memory.

When and where do I find intimacy now? Mostly I think in my intimate memories. Here with you Betty, I feel that I can share my most intimate thoughts and feelings without judgement or condemnation. I have felt intimacy at times when sharing or listening to another's stories. When there is an unspoken agreement that what is shared is confidential. It is intimate and grace to be trusted with another's truth, experiences, and feelings.

At times, like this morning sitting in the stillness under a blue, blue sky watching white puffy clouds drift by, I feel the comfort of a relationship gone now but always with me. A look, a meeting of eyes without words across a crowded room. The holding of hands in the doctor's offices. The simple presence enjoyed on a ride through the fall countryside, are intimate memories. A quiet goodnight.

Closeness, affection, warmth, familiarity, and belonging are words used in conjunction with intimacy. If we think on them for a minute, we can clearly see, Betty, that we may be experiencing intimacy in more places than we imagine and in all of the stages of our one true and amazing life.

With intimacy,

Me

How do you feel about intimacy?

What are some of your fondest intimate moments?

The Intuition Muscle

September 22, 2024

Dear Betty,

I had an intuitive moment today. It's raining for the first time in a couple of weeks. I am happy for a rainy day. Here is what happened. It is Sunday and I would usually get up and get ready to go to church. A rather new experience for me. That is another story. I was having an interior chat with myself about whether I was really going to go or not. Afterall, it was storming and the coffee tasted good. Yet, something inside me was encouraging me to stay in, stay home. I gave in without any sense of guilt or self-scolding.

What happened a bit later is the intuitive affirmation. I received a call from someone who's mom has died and I am going to officiate the Celebration of Life for them. I have been trying to get in touch with him and there he was calling. We had a quick chat and made arrangements to talk later with his brothers. Later, as I began to think about all of the things that we would need to discuss, it occurred to me that had I gone to church out of my sense of what I should have done, I would have missed his call. I trusted my intuition even though I didn't realize that until much later.

Intuition is an interesting phenomenon. It is wonderful too! It can help us find our way through everyday choices. It can help us make choices for ourselves especially now as the questions and experiences that we face in our older years become more and more complicated. As a young woman, I trusted this tool and encouraged others to develop their intuitive muscles as well. Betty, don't you just love the way the words and lessons of our youth somehow find their way back to us. Thank goodness.

Promising to listen and intuit,

Me

How do you imagine that intuition might be a tool?

What fear do you have to face to trust your gift of intuition?

What Was I Thinking?

September 24, 2024

Dear Betty,

Have you ever gotten yourself into a situation or a project, the kind that you jumped in with both feet? Well into it you began to say, "What was I thinking?" Well, Betty, that phrase was pressing on my mind this morning.

It did take a different turn though. In my reverie this morning I was thinking about the way we lived our lives. I don't remember thinking much about what was going to come next. Each day had enough of its own worries and wonders and so one foot in front of the other seemed to be the order of our lives.

At eighty I find myself wondering more often about what I should be thinking about. I am not sure because it is not a pattern that I am used to. My life was cut on other lines, no pattern really. Today I am still putting one foot in front of the other. I focus more on what I am doing rather than what I am thinking. I am a bit more about what I might be feeling on any given day and I guess, that at times gets me to asking again, what was I thinking?

I am doing things that I hope are meaningful and I will confess Betty, in the midst of when life starts moving a little faster than I want to go, I still ask, "What was I thinking?"

Feet still moving,

Me

How do you feel about wondering "What were you thinking?"

Can you remember or share a moment when you asked yourself the same question?

Oops!

September 25, 2024

Dear Betty,

Lately I have noticed that my mind is two steps ahead of my feet. I was getting ready to go out for the day, brushed my teeth, and put drops in my eyes and dots of face cream on my face. Rather than finishing this toilette, I was off and onto getting dressed and choosing which shoes would be the therapeutic best for the long day ahead.

I returned to the bathroom for a little spritz of perfume when I glanced into the mirror and low and behold, I still had the four dots of face cream just waiting to be worked into my aging face. I laughed right out loud Betty. *How silly,* I thought. I must really be losing it now and it is a good thing that I checked the mirror. It would have been a lark if I had gone to the first meeting of the day looking like a clown who forgot to finish the job.

Betty, I think the lesson of the day is this: Always finish the job before taking the next step into whatever or whoever lies ahead. I also think Betty that it is good to learn to laugh at myself because these oops moments seem to be happening more often than not. Or maybe I am just more aware of them since I no longer have anyone to check me out before I go out of the door.

Checking first, going confident,

Me

What is an oops moment that you have enjoyed?

How comfortable are you with not taking yourself too seriously?

When might an oops moment turn into a story that you would be willing to share, letting others know you are a person of good humor?

Effort

September 26, 2024

Dear Betty,

How much effort do I want to give today? Remember when we just got on to our days, knew what we had to do, and doing them didn't take much effort at all? Well, I have been thinking a lot about that lately. I have a clear picture in my mind of taking care of the kids, the house, special holidays, vacations, and many others, oh yes, work, to recall. What I do recall is that everything just got done. I am sure that there was plenty of effort put into it but it was just not something that I thought about. Ah, those were the days!

These days, just getting ready to go to the grocery story can take an amount of effort. Of course, some days are effortless, those would be the ones that find me sitting in my chair watching a movie on Netflix. I believe that all elders should take advantage of an effortless day once in a while. I realize that I am much more intentional in choosing what I want to give effort to, what is it I need at this stage of my life, and what is worth the effort?

Betty, I want you to know that I am so grateful that I can still stand up straight, tie my own shoes if I put my foot on a stool, and all in all continue to be pretty darn independent. So, I guess I should not complain when something requires a bit of effort. I will try to remember just how blessed I am.

No effort today,

Me

How comfortable are you with letting yourself choose what you want to give time and energy into?

What do you consider effort these days?

Going Back

September 28, 2024

Dear Betty,

Going back is different from reverie. For me going back is reaching into my past to visualize just how it was. Usually, Betty, what I find is that the place in my mind is not at all the way it was in my past.

As a small child I lived in what I thought to be a really big building. My parents owned a business on Main Street in a small town in Wisconsin. This building had four apartments upstairs. One of those apartments was ours. I don't have any real sense of what it looked like or which apartment we lived in, just that for a time it was home to me and my two sisters and my mom and dad.

One day I thought it would be interesting to go back to that town and see that building and share that part of my life story with my own family. We lived in a small city not far from that town. I packed a picnic lunch and we were off on an adventure to see where momma lived when she was a child.

Well. Let me tell you Betty, I was in for a real surprise. The building that I thought was so big when I was a child was in reality not big at all. The town? It was just one main street that led down to the railway station. We drove out of town and found a county park where we shared our picnic. I continued to tell my story about the big, big place I lived that wasn't big at all.

I think that it is a good thing to do once in a while, this going back. It gives perspective to us about how our view or reality of our lives change if we take the time to look back and see what was really there. This could be a lesson in life review at this stage of my life. Where have I been and what are the situations or experiences that I thought were so big and insurmountable. They were all part of making me who I am today. Going back was a good thing.

Glad I went,

Me

Where might you go back to see more clearly?

How could going back be helpful to you?

Metaphors

September 29, 2024

Dear Betty,

I really enjoy metaphors. I like to read them and I like to write them but I especially enjoy the feeling I get when one comes to mind that identifies where I am emotionally on any given day.

Seasons are just too easy to use as metaphors. They make so much sense. I have watched three seasons come and go since I started to write to you about my eightieth year. Today I am noticing the subtle changes in the color of the grass, the wind feels just a little different and even the sky is full of fall clouds. The puffy summer clouds that you can dream with and make cloud pictures with seem to be fading.

I am trying hard, Betty, to be disciplined and not use fall or the fall equinox as a way to describe myself today. So, how about this: today I am a squirrel scampering around collecting nuts and seeded grass. I am carefully storing the bounty of the summer. Fall, for me, is time to take in all that summer has gifted me. See that Betty? I just couldn't help myself. Oh, well, all metaphors are good.

Seeking,

Me

Do you see the seasons as words waiting to happen?

How do seasonal metaphors help you explain your feelings or your age journey?

World Keeps Spinning

September 30, 2024

Dear Betty,

Today feels like I wish it was tomorrow. I am sad and a little anxious. I am feeling a little out of control. Getting cozy with change is just a part, although a big part, of aging. I never have felt it as strongly as I have in my eightieth year.

There are so many things that I need to accept. My daughters are nearing their own issues of entering their 60th year. My grandchildren are grown and having families of their own or traveling to see the world or struggling to find their place in their now grown-up life.

I said goodbye to my eldest daughter today. She is leaving for France. It is a lovely thing for her, her daughter and her husband, and her youngest daughter. They will be celebrating a friend's wedding, site seeing, and making memories. I am so happy for them and yet I found myself a bit weepy for the first time in a while.

What is it, I asked? Once again, I do not have an answer. Perhaps it is just an old lady's melancholy about days and times gone by. These reality checks seem to come more frequently lately. I am not sure that I appreciated them at all. No Betty, not at all. My world has changed and that is for sure.

Waiting for tomorrow,

Me

What changes are you feeling uncomfortable with today?

How are you feeling about changes that you cannot control?

OCTOBER

Highs & Lows

October 1, 2024

Dear Betty,

I just couldn't find the way to tell you how I am feeling today. Then I found the following advice and so here it is:

Don't wish me happiness

I don't expect to be happy all the time...

It's gotten beyond that somehow.

Wish me courage and strength and a sense of humor.

I will need them all.

– Anne Morrow Lindbergh

Highs and lows. It seems to me that as I continue on this journey, they become more and more pronounced. When I am happy, I am really happy, but yesterday, I was feeling pretty darn low. I felt like an inner tube with a puncture hole in it slowly sinking in the pool of *"now what?!"*

Then I found the reading and it made sense to me. It is just what I wanted to say, so thank you, Anne Morrow Lindbergh.

This journey into eldering definitely needs regular infusions of courage, strength of body and mind, and a sense of humor when the inner tube springs a leak.

I enjoyed Anne Morrow Lindbergh's book, *Gift of the Sea* years ago. I think I will go back and take another look. It just might give me more tools with which to mend my days of leaking happiness.

Thanks Anne,

Me

What would you describe as your highs and lows?

How would you pack for your journey into your next saga?

Marathon or Sprint

October 2, 2024

Dear Betty

There was a time in my long and productive life in which I could take on the world from dawn to dusk. Whether I was raising kids, canning garden vegetables, getting ready for a holiday, or of course planning a program for work.

These days, I am happy if I can manage a sprint. I am so blessed to have good health, good friends, and a really good family. Still, I find myself offering an excuse for not staying at the party too long or declining a full day's outing, opting instead for a shorter day.

Betty, today while thinking about the idea of a marathon or sprint, I wondered if they applied to my emotional or spiritual life. I guess that I would say that my emotional life has been a marathon. I continue to work to the finish line although I really don't think that there is one. I think that to be healthy I need to always be in touch with my feelings and how they are affecting the rest of me. Spiritual life as a sprint? I confess that at times it has been a marathon, with real determination to stay the course of what I value, my core beliefs. When the walls of my determination feel a bit like an earthquake shaking them, but not crumbling them (thank goodness), it becomes a sprint to get back to the line that I have drawn for, I guess, most of my life.

Cheering me on,

Me

When it comes to your emotional or spiritual life, do you see yourself as a marathon runner or a sprinter?

How does it make you feel knowing that you are heading for the finish line?

Zippers, Buttons, and Necklaces

October 5, 2024

Dear Betty,

Limitations. Each day on the road to elderhood I find more limitations. I can't reach around to zipper up my dress. My fingers don't like to do buttons in small button holes, and if by chance I can get a necklace on, you know for sure Betty that I can not get it off. It is a really good thing that I like it a lot so mostly I just keep wearing it.

What should I do Betty? Here are the choices that I have come up with. I could just whine about these everyday limitations or I could accept the fact that the challenge now is to create new ways to manage these things.

Still, I can tell you that it is not fun trying to learn new strategies for doing the everyday things that used to be so easy. I have also been thinking that it may be a good thing to realize my limitations. This is different from setting boundaries. We will talk about that another time. Realizing my limitations helps me to recognize the reality of this life stage. Yes, there is loss and frustration but there is also a sense of being healthy enough mentally and physically to deal with my limitations. Some days, Betty, taking a good long look at the realities of my life today can be a good thing.

I don't want to waste another day stuck in the 'wish I could' but rather be grateful for 'what I can.'

Helpful hints; don't buy clothes with zippers in the back, pullovers are better than button downs, and when going out with family or friends, simply ask them to help with jewelry.

No zippers today,

Me

How do you feel about your limitations?

What can you do to work through them?

How do you feel about stomping your foot or letting out your frustration in non-hurtful ways?

Quiet Day

October 6, 2024

Dear Betty,

I didn't know what was making me feel uneasy. Not sick or feeling down, just uneasy. What was it? There has been a lot going on lately. Another death in the family and some very bad news for Christy's family. Christy is my middle daughter and her bad news is not related to me really except that it is difficult to see anyone facing a situation that they really cannot do anything about.

Betty, the next three days are full of appointments of one sort or another. A meeting, a family reunion, and a memorial service that I am officiating. While giving myself some time this morning with my comfort cup of coffee, I realized that what I needed was a quiet day. Now I realize that I cannot control the phone ringing or someone dropping in, but I can decide how I will spend this day. I am choosing the quiet.

It is a lovely fall day and I will enjoy it. I will go out into the brisk day with York, sit on the porch, and let my mind be still. Or, I hope that is what will happen. I have come to understand that I need more quiet days now. They are good for me and probably good for my friends and family as well. I find that I am a lot more likable when I have taken the time to listen to my personal needs and actually do something about them.

Being still,

Me

What do you do when you find yourself feeling uneasy?

How do you spend a quiet day, or do you?

Wisdom

October 8, 2024

Dear Betty,

Betty, do you remember the song, "I am Woman, Hear Me Roar?" Do you ever recall hearing another woman say, "I am Wisdom, Hear My Words?" I am beginning to believe that wisdom appears just when you need it. Here I go again, back to definitions. I don't know what I would do if there weren't dictionaries.

Wisdom:

1. *the quality of having experience, knowledge, and good judgment; the quality of being wise.*

"Listen to his words of wisdom" - Oxford Languages Dictionary

It seems to me that I might acknowledge that I have had many experiences in my life. I have gained knowledge and, I hope, good judgement. I gravel with the idea of being wise or having words of wisdom. Still, it is what olders are supposed to have isn't it? I find that having it and acknowledging it are two different things.

The other evening, I had a visitor. He is in the middle of a difficult situation. I was surprised to see him but happy for the company. After a bit of chit chat, he started to tell me about his worries. I listened and I hoped to offer him some words of consolation. I suppose that I was drawing on my experience and knowledge so wisdom, I guess. Why is it so hard for us to name our gifts? Is it false humility or low self-esteem? Maybe neither, maybe it's cultural. Back to the old, "be seen and not heard".

Wherever you land on the word or meaning of wisdom, know that it did feel affirming to think that I could help this young person. I'd like to think that these many years of my life have had purpose and meaning, that they were worth it.

Wisdom, Be it.

Me

How do you see yourself practicing wisdom?

What do you find challenging about naming yourself wise?

Words

October 9, 2024

Dear Betty,

Just as there are memories that we wish we could forget, there are times when I wish I could retrieve words that I have spoken. While I was contemplating this thought, I began to wonder if there were words that I regret not saying.

Of course, we all have questions that we wish we had asked. Things that we would like to know about our families past or Betty, the ones that we ask ourselves. Should I have stayed in that job? What have I done to make you step away from our relationship? How would you have handled this situation, Mom, if you were still here?

I have thought a fair amount about things that I regret in my long and interesting life but until today or the last few days, I have not thought much about words that I regret not saying.

So, for the record, I regret not saying words of support when I could have encouraged a friend. I regret not saying more endearing words to my children. I regret not saying more interesting words to my grandchildren. But, Betty, I really regret not saying I love you to my loved one or to myself for that matter.

Words matter and I hope that I will be more willing to say them when the occasion arises.

Finding words,

Me

What words do you regret not saying?

How will you use your words now?

Will you make different choices about when to use them?

Emotional Noise

October 14, 2024

Dear Betty,

While trying to decide what I was feeling today, I came across a new phrase for myself. Emotional noise is a notion that I think I can reflect on for a while. I have been feeling like something is missing for me emotionally, like I have lost something, but I don't know what it is. Now I wonder if there is just so much emotional noise going on inside me that I can't hear or feel the missing part.

So here is a definition that I think will help me figure this out. Emotional noise *"describes how a person's emotional state can disrupt communication and make it difficult to achieve goals."* - Tyrone Holmes, *Understanding Noise*

The other day I went to a meeting. It was a meeting to discuss a project that I think is interesting and important. The people there were going to discuss ways to support the art community in their area. I had been feeling a little torn about going to the meeting because there had been a lot of things going on in the past few days. We had just learned about another death in the family, I have been preparing the memorial service for a dear friend of mine, and then there is just life in general.

Being a faithful participant however, I went to the meeting because I thought that I should. As I sat there waiting for the meeting to get started, I began to feel like it just wasn't where I wanted to be. I felt disconnected from the conversation and just couldn't get invested in it. I finally left before the meeting got started. So, in this case the emotional noise that I was feeling kept me from achieving my goal of supporting this newly formed group. Still, Betty, I felt so strongly that I needed to leave that I didn't feel any impetus to stay. Maybe I was just too emotionally tired or physically tired or both. I think that I will be paying more attention to my emotional noise in the future.

Listening for the noise,

Me

What do you think about the idea of exploring emotional noise for yourself?

How might you describe your emotional noise?

What experiences have you had that you could count as affected by emotion?

Docile vs. Bad Ass

October 15, 2024

Dear Betty,

Yesterday I was dealing with emotional noise. Today I believe that I have found my missing piece. This has led me to find the definitions of docile and badass and now I need to decide which of these women I want to be.

If you behave well and do what people tell you to do, you're a docile person. Some synonyms are amenable and compliant. (Vocabulary.com.)

If you are a badass, you might be difficult to deal with, mean tempered or tough. You might also be assertive or independent. You might be or think of yourself as awesome or impressive.

I have left my image of myself as docile in the rear-view mirror. Badass? Maybe Betty. Still, I do not think that I am mean tempered or tough. I do think of myself as assertive and somewhat independent. I do not find myself to be awesome or impressive, but then on the other hand I do think that at times I have been both of these things.

So, Betty, I promise that I will try to behave well and keep all of the positive aspects of a badass in my tool bag. Maybe that will help me the next time I am reacting to my emotional noise.

Not so bad,

Me

Can you see yourself as a badass? When and how?

How do you feel about being docile?

Self-Assured vs. Self-confident

October 16, 2024

Dear Betty,

I wrote to you the other day about feeling like I was missing something. If I could use the analogy of myself being a puzzle, I was missing one of my pieces. No Betty, I don't mean that I was losing my mind, I was just not feeling whole.

Now just a few days later, I think I have found my missing piece. I shared my feeling with a friend and she said, "maybe you are just not feeling confident." I respect her assessment but it just didn't resonate with me. I started to think about what else came close to confidence. The answer that came to me was a lack of self-assuredness.

To be self-assured has to do with our inner feelings. It has to do with how we are feeling or experiencing our emotions, how we are physically and spiritually. To be self-confident has to do with things outside of ourselves. It has to do with our skills and talents. It has to do with what we have learned from our lived experiences. Betty, I want to tell you that I have plenty of self-confidence. I have been well-affirmed when it comes to my ability to use my gifts, my skills.

When I felt that I had lost a piece of my innermost being it felt odd and it made me feel sad. Lots of old tapes started playing in my head. I didn't feel comfortable in the situation, like I didn't belong or like the conversation that was happening was one that I probably had way too many years ago. I suppose I felt a little lost, not out of my depth, just not belonging. It almost felt like grief again.

Emotions just happen, they are triggered by so many things.

Being self-assured for me means that I am willing to acknowledge whatever I am feeling on any given day and deal with it. When I am self-assured, I can be more self-confident. If I am at ease emotionally, physically, and spirituality, I can focus on doing the best that I can with my gifts and talents.

When I am not feeling self-assured, I begin to doubt myself and the value of my skills and gifts.

After some quiet reflection and some really good conversation with my wise women friends, I have my piece back now and I am feeling pretty darn self-assured about my emotional, physical, and spiritual wellbeing, Betty, today I think that others invested in the aging process might feel like I did. We olders really have to support our peers when they feel like they have lost a piece of the puzzle.

Picture whole again,

Me

How do you get your pieces back when you feel like you have lost one of them?

What do you do to check in order to see if the whole picture is present?

Being self-assured is an inside job but do you think we can lose a piece of ourselves when we are less self-confident about using our gifts and talents?

Long Shadows

October 19, 2024

Dear Betty,

Part of this aging journey is sad. It is sad because we begin to lose our dear family and friends. Recently, though, I have been thinking about one of my long-time friends who left me with many interesting and provocative ideas. One of our conversations was centered around her saying that one of the things that she liked about the season of fall was the long shadows.

Today I find that I appreciate the memory of this conversation. Since I cannot help myself when it comes to using nature as a metaphor for my life, Betty, I wonder how long shadows fit my story. Well, I see that the length of the shadows depends on the angle of the sun. The shadows also change direction as the day goes on. In the spring, the shadows are shallow. They are longer in summer but at their longest in the fall.

Now Betty, I am thinking that my life story as told by reflecting on shadows would go something like this: the shadows are my life experiences. They are just getting started in the spring of my life when the shadows are short. My middle years see me having more experiences and the shadows are a bit longer and maybe even a little darker. But, in the fall of my years now, the shadows seem to me to be another way to think about my memories. They change direction as there is more light given to them. They are long now because I have lived a good, interesting, and challenging life. Yes, Betty there are some times that I remember the darker shadows. I can say that I have faced most of them down and am at rest with my progress.

I wish I had taken more time to have a deeper conversation with my friend about why she liked long shadows so much. I guess I will just be glad for the memory and the metaphor that her vision gave me.

Searching out my long shadows,

Me

What do you think about this analogy?

What might long shadows mean to you?

How do you think about shadows in your life?

Last Kid on the Playground

October 21, 2024

Dear Betty,

Today I got out of my warm and cozy bed and while enjoying my coffee thought, "I don't have to do anything," today. I couldn't think of anything that I should do or that I, "for sure" had to do. I tried to put words or a picture together of what I was feeling. The best I could do was to say that I felt like the last kid standing on the playground after everyone else had been chosen to play the game. What is the game that everyone is playing?

Having had the experience of not being chosen at times in my life, I didn't like to be reminded of those feelings again. I am old after all and there are many days that I simply do not want to play any game.

Truthfully Betty, I am beginning to wonder if I will ever get used to this new way of being. Will I ever get used to having nothing to do, no have to's, not even one should? Maybe I would have been better equipped for this life stage if I had spent more time sitting on the porch at the end of the day like my aunties. I am grateful though for the memories of how I see them being happy and content with their lives. Do you think I am romanizing?

Well Betty, there are many days that are still full and I am still seeing other people and engaging in meaningful conversation. No doubt about it, I am blessed. Maybe I will try to embrace the little girl standing alone on the playground. Instead of being sad or lonely about the game, I will try to see what the new game in town is and learn how to play it. Or not!

Ready, set, play,

Me

P.S. When I finished writing to you Betty, I took York, my energetic border collie out for some exercise. While waiting for him to take his usual run around I began to think about the day I wrote to you about. This brought me back to remembering when, in my fifties, there were some days whose meetings were cancelled, or we had snow days. I celebrated these days. I was so happy for a day to stay at home and do whatever I wanted to do. Do you think that this might be the answer, Betty? Maybe I need to think about these days as a gift and celebrate them. A little gratitude would not go amiss. Maybe I need to give myself permission to do whatever I want, whatever that may be.

What do you think about the game people play at eighty?

How do you cope when you feel like the last kid on the playground?

What might you do if you know someone who feels like that?

When?

October 22, 2024

Dear Betty,

Today I am feeling a bit melancholy. I am wondering just when I began to think about aging or becoming an older. In my late fifties many of my friends were turning sixty. It was the time when women had become pretty self-sufficient and exploring just what that meant. Stepping out of ancient stereotypes can be daunting.

There were books being written and movies filmed. One of the books that had a big impact on the women in my circle was the book, *The Divine Secrets of the Ya Ya Sisterhood.* It was about a small circle of women who stepped out of their assigned roles to do things that they never did when they were younger. Another influence about that same time was the idea of becoming a Crone when one turned sixty. It was just another way of trying to name or to become who we might be at this life stage. There were Croning ceremonies, probably influenced by the Ya Ya book.

This was probably the time when I first started to think about being older. We laughed and celebrated and danced around firepits. All with the hope that we might become a little wiser as we aged. Of course, after the bonfire and the wine bottles were empty, we returned to our homes and lives. Off to work the next morning or trying to think about what to make for dinner or the potluck at the kid's school.

I went on to work at the Wisconsin Rural Women's Initiative trying to empower farm and rural women. Betty, I just didn't give much thought to what was to come or where I might be in ten or twenty years. Now, here I am trying to get a grip on this decade that is ever present with me. Writing to you has helped me come to at least some understanding about being eighty. I think that there is much more learning ahead for me and with you here with me, I will manage it with grace and wisdom. Thanks Ya Ya's.

When is now,

Me

How much time have you spent thinking about becoming older?

What influences do you think are important to your aging process?

Feeble, Fragile, Wrinkled, Not Me

October 23, 2024

Dear Betty,

There was a time when I thought that a woman of 60 or 70 but mostly eighty would appear feeble or fragile. Moving slowly, probably using a walking stick. She would have a wrinkled face and her hands would be veined. She might eat slowly and speak with a soft voice or not much at all. She would shuffle around the house and I would hope that she wouldn't stumble on the throw rugs that had been in her house for years and years.

Well Betty, here I am. I am eighty plus and I hope that I do not appear at all the way I, in my earlier years, perceived an older woman. I am standing tall, even though I am only four foot eleven inches, I don't see myself presenting as feeble, or fragile. I own my wrinkles but do confess that I slather face cream on generously, using more that I am sure prescribed. My hair is white and I no longer wear fancy shoes with three-inch heels. How do the young women manage to walk in them Betty?

Isn't it interesting how our perception changes with age? I used to enjoy the images of older women that are supposed to be funny. Did they influence my view of aging women? The description of the woman is not at all what my experience of older women has been. I don't recall the aunties ever seeming to me to be that description. I am engaged now with women who look like me. We still wear jeans and a little makeup sometimes. We are independent, and I do not detect any shuffling as yet. Will we become the woman I described today? To some extent I suppose that we will, or will we say, "oh no, not me." A time will come Betty, I know it will, when acceptance will knock on my door once again. I will deal with it then, for now I celebrate and am grateful for this day. And, Betty, I do still have a sense of humor about being eighty.

Not feeble yet,

Me

What is your image of an older woman?

What image do you have of yourself in the aging process?

What do you think about the idea of acceptance knocking on your door when it comes to your personal image of yourself?

Quiet Turns to Noise

October 24, 2024

Dear Betty,

This week has been quiet. I was called for jury duty and even though I didn't have to appear, I had to clear my calendar for the week. Not that there is much on it these days anyway. Today I found myself sitting in the quiet. The T.V. was off, no music playing, no audible book teaching me anything. Just quiet. What happened next led me to the title for today's missive.

At times I find that when I let myself sit in the quiet, my mind starts to rewind phrases that seemed relevant at the time or conversations that I have long forgotten. It is like what's that phrase? "Oh, yes, old tapes playing." This is when my quiet turns to noise. By noise I mean something that is annoying, different than a word longed for.

Here is the paradox Betty: I have longed for quiet. A quiet mind, a quiet heart, and. a quiet spirit. A sense of just being comfortable in my own skin: another modern phrase, I think. Now at this time of my life, I do appreciate quiet most days, but on some others, noise creeps in and I want to ignore it. I am not so sure that this is helpful to my process. Perhaps part of the elder's process is being brave enough to acknowledge the noise, embrace it, and hopefully learn the lessons that it is trying to teach.

Listening to Noise,

Me

*Do you experience noise in your mind when practicing
"quiet"?*

What do you feel when your quiet turns to noise?

How do you respond to old tapes playing?

Life Keeps Rewinding at 80

October 25, 2024

Dear Betty,

While taking a walk through our past letters, I came across one titled "Quiet."

Funny, I thought since I just wrote to you yesterday about quiet and noise. What do I think is funny about this, Betty? It made me think that it is the way of this life stage, isn't it? We just keep doing the same things over and over. Well maybe not doing the same things but perhaps feeling and thinking the same things over and over.

I feel like a child who has to learn to memorize. That's how they learn. Each time I find myself contemplating the same words or experiences I tend to see them in a different light. This made me wonder if the sun shines in the exact same place or in the exact same way every day? Clearly not because it is impacted by clouds, rain, storms, and weather of all kinds. It is also impacted by how the environment around us changes. Gardens are planted, trees cut down, parks created. You get the picture, Betty.

So now that I have looked at the word or experience of "quiet" in a new light, I can't wait to see how many more times I will find new lessons to add to my experience of aging. Oh my, does this mean that I will keep re-winding all of the others written about? We will just have to wait and see.

Re-playing,

Me

What do you think about my experience of writing about the same thing twice?

What happens when you find yourself experiencing the same situation over and over again?

What do you find worth re-winding or re-playing?

Routine

October 26, 2024

Dear Betty,

Life is different now Betty, for so many years there was a routine to my daily existence. Each decade brought new time schedules, things that had to be done at home, children cared for, and belonging to a community. Each of these things meant some semblance of order or I might say routine.

These days I feel like a lot of loose ends are swirling around, maybe a little like a spider web that has come undone but not let go completely. Will I ever find a routine that I can be comfortable with? That will spin a web that feels like home, comfort, peace? Actually Betty, I feel like I am getting closer to finding the center, relaxing into ordinary days, but open to the spontaneous ones as well.

It is hard for those of us trying to decipher life in the eighties. It is hard to let go of old habits. It is hard to step back out of old routines and be brave enough to find new ones. Betty, life is challenging in so many ways now but almost exciting too.

No routine needed,

Me

How do you feel about finding new routines as you age?

Have you noticed that your routines have changed through the years? How has that been for you?

What would you like to change in your routine life now?

Wanderlust

October 28, 2024

Dear Betty,

As often happens these days, I found myself stuck in a memory about one of my uncles. I rarely saw him and have no idea where he might be now, but one thing I do remember was my mom saying often, "Your Uncle John has the wonderlust. He can't stay in one place long at all." Of course, this memory took me on my own travels through definitions to try and gain some understanding of the word.

Wanderlust is a strong desire to wander or travel and explore the world. Most of us experience the wish to visit faraway places once in a while, recently overseas trips are being replaced with staycations! This feeling is so familiar that we have a special word for it, Wanderlust, sometimes spelt Wunderlust. "It represents that urge to break from everyday life and experience something new and unknown." (Wikipedia.)

My granddaughter Tess, has definitely grown the Wanderlust gene. She is a nurse who hopes to become a traveling nurse in the near future. She loves to travel and has no fear of doing it at all. She uses every opportunity to explore her world near and far. I think that she is amazing and has more than enough hutzpah to make it happen.

I am grateful for the amount of travel that I have enjoyed in my life. Now, however, I am happy to take the last line of the definition, "the urge to break from everyday life and experience something new and unknown," right here in my cozy comfy chair or rocking on the back porch. I have decided that I will make the other spelling of the word work for me. Wanderlust is something that I can confess to. I wonder a lot. I wonder what is happening in my world, I wonder how long I have to be healthy and happy, I wonder about my children and grandchildren, what will their lives hold for them? I wonder if those I have lost really knew how much I cared for, loved, them. And on and on it goes. I see that I do suffer wanderlust.

About breaking from everyday life and experiencing something new and unknown, I can say it is true. I am doing things that surprise me and that I am proud of, for instance becoming an author, joining a new faith community and moving on from what others think I should be doing to what I am called to do or be.

God bless the travelers,

Me

What is your understanding of wanderlust?

How have you experienced the urge to be a traveler?

Where do your wonder days take you?

The Sun will Rise

October 29, 2024

Dear Betty,

I am sure that I have heard this phrase before but somehow today it held my attention. I was watching a show on T.V. The person was having a difficult time and another person said, what are you going to do if you don't get any help? The first person said, "Tomorrow, the sun will still rise." Yes, I said to myself, it will in spite of me or my gloomy attitude. What a hopeful way to think about life, I thought.

I think that it is one of those things that I need to copy and put on my mirror. I need to be reminded often that I am doing my best to walk through these un-chartered waters we call aging. Still, remembering that whatever happens in my life, the sun will still rise and the moon will set on another day, and I am called to practice hope. If not for myself, then at least for everyone else.

Tomorrow morning, I will see the sun rise and even if it is cloudy, I will know it is rising somewhere. I will look forward to watching the orange harvest moon appear over the pasture and once again I will find hope.

Basking in the sunshine,

Me

What do you think about this way of seeing hope?

How do you find hope these days?

What metaphors might be helpful to you?

Waste a Day

October 30, 2024

Dear Betty,

It seems to me that women of a certain age struggle with realizing a day without anything on the calendar. This week I have had several days wide open. Each morning while having my coffee, I try my best to take a breath and to stop thinking of all of the things that I could or should do. Why is it so hard to do nothing Betty?

Is it wasteful to just be quiet and still? Is it wasteful to take the time, ah there you have it, the idea that to just do nothing is a waste of time? Time becomes a large issue when one is in the delightful stage of eldering. For those of us who grew up in a family of "waste not want not", mentally the idea of spending a day, taking the time, for one self was just not done.

It has not been easy to practice being alright with days that let me ponder just exactly what it is that I want to do and not what I think I have to do. Being still however, listening to the wind chimes on the back porch or the flocks of geese heading off and away has at times brought me the most creative ideas.

Now, as I am writing this to you Betty, I realize that I just shared my doings in a day that I will not count as wasteful. Listening, pondering ideas, and being still are doings.

Waste a day, Betty. Let yourself just be and let the doings present themselves in a way that lets you make the choice about what to do with them. Watch a movie that you have wanted to see, take a long walk, do some art, or write a letter to your best friend. Maybe just do nothing. After making your choice, let me know if you think that your time or your day was a waste.

Good wasting,

Me

What will happen if you take time to waste a day?

How do you feel about having a clear calendar? Does it make you feel anxious?

How will you celebrate taking a day off, wasting a day?

View Master

October 31, 2024

Dear Betty,

Being eighty is like holding a view master and looking at each picture remembering each one before pushing down the lever to present the next one. This image came to me as I was wondering why our aging minds click through our memories, usually the oldest first. Why Betty, do we find ourselves sifting through the oldest stuff of our lives instead of focusing on the present? Do you think they have view master discs for the future?

You do know what a view master is, don't you? It is a small plastic thing that looks like a binocular but that you look through with both eyes. There is a place on the front of it that holds a disc filled with tiny pictures that are enlarged when you look through it. You click through each picture one at a time unlike today's podcasts or videos.

My mom bought me a disc each time I went to the dentist and behaved myself. Betty, I thought of this today because I am feeling a bit melancholy. I wish I had a view master that I could look into and see all of the good times I have had, the people I have loved, and the things that I have done.

So, Betty, if eighty is like a view master it is holding my life story. And just like the disc that goes around and around as many times as you push the lever, then eighty is like a view master. When I am open and ready to look and see the pictures of my past, I can choose to stay engaged there or I can realize how I have changed and grown. I can and have changed the disc. I am strong and capable and carrying on. Appreciating the memories and the love but today is another day on my road to whatever.

Engaged,

Me

What pictures would you like to see in your view master?

How do memories present themselves to you and how do you respond?

November

Personality

November 1, 2024

Dear Betty,

Today, Betty, I am feeling confident. I have been asking myself what this whole year has been about. Is it a journey worth taking? It was and is, I think. Trying to decipher the meaning of life at eighty has been difficult at times and confounding at others. Today I believe that what I have been struggling with all along is the difference between what our culture tells us about aging and my own thoughts and feelings. Well, I think that has been part of it.

How much does our personality fit into the telling of our stories? Today I am feeling confident in my belief that I have been true to my aspirations of being authentic, eccentric, and wise. If I am not willing to take a look into the kaleidoscope of my life through my personality, I am not being authentic. Today I think that it is important to dissect what is our character, our natural way of being.

I am an introvert although many people do not believe that of me. They judge me by my persona. Yes Betty, I have done many things that would lead others to think that I am an extrovert. I like to say, "I can show up when I need to." My preference though, especially now at eighty, is to be on my own. I am most authentic in my own space and engaged with my own thoughts. I am working at the eccentric piece of how I want to be perceived and at various times over the past two decades I have been thought of as being a little bit wise.

Betty, I am sure that my letters over these last several months have come out sounding like my personal need for understanding. At times I have wished for a clear path to the rest of my days. Still, I do not want to change the way we are traveling together. Writing to you has given me much insight, affirmation and for sure much to think about. I wonder if I go back through our letters, I would find a lot to learn about my personality. And maybe yours too!

Personally yours,

Me

Have you thought much about your personality and how it affects your daily life?

How is your personality different from your persona or have you blended them into your authentic self?

Not OK

November 3, 2024

Dear Betty,

There are many things that I think about when I think about what is not OK. Things like ageism or all of the other "isms". But Betty, there are enough books, articles, podcasts research to be had if one wants that kind of information. Today I want to tell you about how I feel, really, authentically.

When I was engaged in Don's journey through his last three years, I would accompany him to the doctors. Many doctors. The team would come into the tiny room where we had been waiting and they would look at him and ask, "How are you today, Don?" He would usually reply with something like, "I am still standing upright," or "except for my back, knee, shoulder etc. I am doing alright." Then they would look at me and ask the same question. My usual reply was, I am OK.

Today, Betty, I want to tell you that I am not OK. For the last week or so I have been feeling sad and small, unnoticed. Writing this makes me feel like a "poor me" again. But it is the truth. I don't know why but tears have reappeared at the most unexpected moments. They make themselves noticed while watching either a sad or uplifting story on the news. I have had the embarrassing presence in a conversation that was about a memory of Don and Dre and other recent losses.

I have been told that the second year of a loss is better, that things will be better. Ha, I say. Not only is this the second year of his passing but the first year of my eighties journey. Well, this could explain feeling sad but what about small and unnoticed? Maybe it is because I am seen now as only half of a presence, smaller somehow without him. Most times I like being unnoticed these days but is that really me being authentically me? Betty, I feel like I am being silly. I am, after all, continuing the work that I have always done. I am writing, facilitating, mothering, grandmothering, and being a friend and part of a community.

It is cloudy today; I think I am just having a cloudy-feeling day. If you asked me today, "How are you?"

I think I would say, "I am not OK." Tomorrow I may be just fine and do you know what Betty? I will still be eighty.

Not OK but alright,

Me

How truthful are you about your feelings?

What is it that keeps us from sharing our true feelings?

Never Stop Becoming

November 4, 2024

Dear Betty,

I suppose that I should be writing about the election that is happening tomorrow. Like most of my friends, I just don't even want to think about it and what the consequences might be. It makes me sad because in my youth I was interested in our country's presidential election. Now I am fearful and sad, so I am going to share other thoughts with you today. I did, however, vote early.

For most of my adult life I encouraged people, young people, middle aged people, and old people to be all that they could be, the best of themselves. I talked about accepting ourselves and to never stop becoming. In those years of teaching, facilitating, and commiserating with other like-minded people, it seemed a good choice to make. We could see progress, we affirmed one another, challenged one another and watched as T.V. talk shows were taking on the mantle of self-discovery, becoming.

Betty, I know that we have seen and heard all of the old cliches about looking in the mirror and asking who the reflection of ourselves was and how did we get that way? So many others I don't want to mention here. What comes to me now as I take a good look at myself is this, "It is the same package with better contents." Acceptance is a never-ending ribbon that wraps around us over and over again. Too bad it doesn't present sometimes with a pretty bow.

Now I wonder what "becoming" means to me at eighty. More often than not I might ask, "not how or who am I becoming, but rather what will become of me." Over these months, Betty, I have shared so many learnings with you. I have shared challenges and asked questions that I have only some answers for. I think this process is helping me become the best that I can be. It sure has helped my spelling and language acuity.

I will confess that I am not happy with the image I say good morning to each day. There is no going back; I am not the plastic surgery type. I am going to try accepting each new droop and wrinkle as an important part of my becoming. My hope is that I will be looked upon as a well-weathered, kind, and curious older whose insides still do not match her outsides, but who continues to be willing to seek becoming.

Always becoming,

Me

How do you feel about the ongoing journey of becoming?

What is your image of yourself?

How difficult is it for you to accept the you that you are today?

I'm Back

November 5, 2024

Dear Betty,

Yesterday I sat myself down and had a heart-to-heart talk with myself. "Get a grip," I said. "You have just as many choices today as you had yesterday and the day before that. Why are you choosing to take the path of woe is me?" I guess we all have cloudy-feeling days sometimes.

Each day has 24 hours. No more and no less. It is what I decide to do with my 24 hours that matters. I can go through the list of what if's, woulda, shoulda, coulda or I can try my best to live in the present moment. I may not know what tomorrow will bring but today I can enjoy the time to listen to myself think. I heard a quote the other day from Matthew Hicks. David Begnaud did an interview with him. Matt is a homeless man who plays his guitar and literally sings for his supper. Here are his words of wisdom, "Expression can take you out of depression."

No Betty, I am not depressed but I do have some, "feeling down" moments. I hope that I can remember to be grateful each day for at least a few of the minutes of my 24 hours for a positive thought of the past rather than the what if's. Here is more of the wisdom of Matt, "Expression can give you peace, doing something for others, I want it (his expression through music) to mean something." Finally, he said, "What sets your soul on fire?"

I leave you with that thought today Betty in search of what sets my soul on fire. I will keep you posted.

Blessing the day,

Me

What sets your soul on fire?

What is your prescription for days when you are "feeling down?"

Taking the By-Pass

November 7, 2024

Dear Betty,

If I think about my eightieth year as a journey then I posit that I could imagine myself traveling on a highway. I am not sure of the destination as yet but I hope that it is one of understanding. Along the way I experience road signs that help me ponder things like my feelings, hopes, and memories.

Today, Betty, I found a bypass and I decided to take it. The bypass said, turn here for a mood check. Am I taking this metaphor too far Betty? Oh well, let's follow it a bit longer. Perhaps checking my mood and leaving the highway of feelings, hopes, and memories for a minute I might find that my mood or the way in which I present my aura to others moves me to a deeper understanding of where I have been and where I might be headed.

I am in a fairly good mood today. I slept well, the sun is shining, and even though I am not happy with the outcome of the election, the commercials on the T.V. are back to fast food and lawyers. Betty, I am not saying that I am not in touch with my deeper feelings, just that I am enjoying a lighter mood, a happier one and I hope that I can honestly say, "today I am in a good mood, not just fairly good but solidly good.

Maybe I should take the bypass more often.

Bypassing,

Me

What might be a bypass that you would consider taking?

How does your mood affect the way in which you interact with others?

How do you relate to the often used phrase, "Glass half full, glass half empty, another metaphor for mood?"

Flexible vs. Spontaneous

November 9, 2024

Dear Betty,

This idea to write to you today about being flexible vs. being spontaneous came to me as I was bending down to tie my shoes. For the last few days, I have been noticing that I do bend fairly well. I bend down to pick up York's dish, I bend down to put on my shoes, I bend to pick up his toys. I bend.

I am grateful for my flexibility, even though there are other ways in which I am not so flexible or bendable. You know, Betty, it's those "I can get down moments but if I do get down, will I be able to get up again?" Not so flexible in that situation.

All of this reminded me of a time when Don came home from work and wanted to take our three little girls and me to the local ice cream stand for a treat. I said, "I have to finish the dishes and get the girls ready for bed, etc.

He said, "Those things will still be here when we get back. Come on, it's a lovely night."

I guess that in this case I was not very flexible or spontaneous. I have since accepted the challenge or willingness to say yes and at times just go with the flow. Being physically flexible will continue to be a challenge but I am much more open to the idea of being more flexible mentally. I am not sure that my kids would agree.

Well Betty, we did go out for ice cream. Don did encourage my spontaneity throughout our life together. He was a master at going with the flow, except when the flow created a dam around his character or values.

Back to flexibility. Because I can say that I am pretty good at being spontaneous, I don't see that changing much just because I am eighty. I do find however, that I find myself being or at least trying to be flexible. There are so many things that change when we reach the middle years. There are only more challenges to adapt to new ways of being, learning, and staying as flexible as possible.

Bendable,

Me

Do you see yourself as spontaneous or flexible at your stage of life?

What is your history of being either spontaneous or flexible?

Gratitude Not Cliché

November 11, 2024

Dear Betty,

I decided that when I wrote to you today, I wanted to be more positive. It seems that I have not shared much about the many things for which I am grateful. As usual Betty, the more I contemplated what I wanted to say to you the more I found myself asking, "Why don't I, like so many others, get on the gratitude bandwagon." Cliché, I thought.

So of course, I had to find the true meaning of a cliché. Here you go!

"A cliché is a phrase that, due to overuse, is seen as lacking in substance or originality." - Litchart.com

We come up with or hear someone else use a phrase that sounds clever and we use it and use it until we get tired of hearing it. Then it loses its appeal. I am sure that you can think of one or two. "Actions speak louder than words." About gratitude, "have an attitude of gratitude." Not a bad thing to have but after a while hearing it in a way that is meant to give us a directive because of course we just couldn't figure out by ourselves that being grateful is a good idea.

I can also practice being appreciative, thankful, humbled, indebted, but they are just not as clever as having an attitude of gratitude. It is a really meaningful cliché even if I am afraid it has lost some of its umph. I am going to try changing up my list to what I appreciate that makes me feel grateful. Plain old thank you might not go amiss.

Are these word games part of my signature here in the reality of my eightieth year? They do keep me questioning and learning Betty. So sorry if today was still a bit too cranky.

Indebted and blessed,

Me

How do you feel about clichés?

What is your go-to cliché?

Do you think gratitude as a cliché is overused? What would you replace it with?

Ties That Bind

November 16, 2024

Dear Betty,

It was sometime between waking up and really trying to go back to sleep that I had this random memory. I heard Don asking "Where is your mom?" I remember exactly where I was the night he asked.

"I am right here," I said from the kitchen.

What are the ties that bind us to our loved ones? What are the ties that bind us to anyone who is no longer in our realm? I believe now after some time of loss that what ties us to them or to experiences from our past are the random thoughts or memories that just barge into our consciousness or our dreams when we least expect it. Betty, I remember one of these ties that have me bound forever from my friend Susan. After one of our outings to an antique mall, we got into the car and as we settled in, she said, "Well that was underwhelming." I think of this always; it is a tie I will not ever forget.

Betty, I wonder what other ties we might have that keep us bound to others? Besides memories, I believe that some of who they were becomes part of us. They might have changed our way of thinking about something. Perhaps there are things that we learned through great conversations or even just good times shared.

Ties that bind are important to me and the idea has given me yet something else to explore through these new years. Betty, is legacy part of what creates ties that bind?

All tied up,

Me

How would you describe "ties that bind"?

What do you think about memories as ties that bind?

Are we creating ties that bind as we strive to be healthy and wise elders?

Gift to Be Simple

November 19, 2024

Dear Betty,

Yesterday I met with my health insurance agent. He is a kind and good man who has made sure that Don and I always had the best plan for us, even when Don was terribly sick.

After he left, I was thinking about how I was feeling. Usually, you know Betty, this kind of taking care of business would make me anxious or at least uncomfortable. He has a way of making me feel safe and cared for. But what I really want to tell you is this, I was thinking that what I thought was going to be complicated turned out to be simple.

Simple, I thought, an interesting idea. I have been feeling pretty comfortable in myself these last few weeks. I noticed that even though I was taking care of things that I don't care to do, it felt simple. Now Betty, I am wondering how much of the time in this eighties journey I have been making a mountain out of a molehill? I like the idea of looking through the glass of simplicity.

It is a gift. If I can remain in the space of seeing things more simply, or at least as not overwhelming, I feel calm and even a little smart and forward looking. I read a book once written by author Sue Bender titled

Plain and Simple, A Journey to the Amish. The author stayed with an Amish family for six weeks to come to an understanding of them and their lifestyle. One of the lessons that she shared was the idea of "finishing one thing and then moving on." I can't tell you how many times since I read that book, which was a long time ago, that I have used that lesson. Sometimes I think we look at things that we view as simple and we want more noise, more color, more discussion, more dissention, more chaos. At eighty I am looking forward to holding on to this newfound gift and letting my life be simple. Actually, I find that it makes me feel more aware and awake to my world. I can see clearly now. Hopefully tomorrow as well.

Gifted,

Me

How do you feel about being gifted with simplicity?

What in your life could you work to simplify?

If you don't like the idea of living simply, what would you choose in place of it?

Blessed or Bereft?

November 20, 2024

Dear Betty,

It seems to me that one way to describe my life these days is to say that on one hand I feel really really blessed and on the other I am feeling bereft. I decided that I would look up the definitions of these two words even though I was sure I knew what they meant. I wonder how many words I take for granted are like this? Well, that will be another exploration.

So here we go Betty, two different meanings. I had forgotten that blessed another form of blest is used in mild expressions of annoyance or exasperation. Example: There wasn't a blessed thing anybody could have done, I was not blest with the answer.

Today I like this definition better; bringing pleasure, contentment, or good fortune. Betty, don't you think that it better describes a greater part of our lives? I have been blessed with good health, a good family, good friends, good experiences, and more. I have felt more contentment than angst and there have been times of pleasure for sure.

Until this year, I don't know if I ever thought much about being bereft. It was not a usual part of my personal lexicon. After looking at the definition of bereft, I see that there are times when in fact I am feeling bereft. Here are just a few of the examples or meanings of the word bereft: "deprived of, robbed of, stripped of, cut off from, parted from." Betty, seeing the word described this way helped me to understand that at times I suppose I have felt all of them. I feel like they put words to the many losses that are experienced in our older years.

I hope that I will remember to accept my times of feeling bereft and then hold them up to the times that I feel incredibly blessed.

Blessed and Bereft,

ME

Are there words that you have found to describe your feelings and thoughts as an elder that you will add to your personal lexicon?

What are they?

How do you feel about exploring blessed and bereft at the same time?

Wisdom? Maybe

November 21, 2024

Dear Betty,

It is a cold and blustery day. The first snow of the season is letting us know that in fact winter has arrived. Kindreds would have met today, but I decided to cancel our gathering because, well Betty, you know why. It is a snowy, stormy day.

Last night I was spending some time just thinking. Thinking about why I am responding to the ordinary events of my life in the way that I have been. It feels like the same kind of feeling I had when I just knew that it was time to start writing to you. Was it intuition? I wondered. Then I came around to this new thought, I have been striving for authenticity and I feel like I have accomplished it, at least most of the time. I thought about my goal of eccentricity. (I still have a way to go with that one.) Wisdom, could it be that this is what WISDOM feels like? A kind of quiet knowing.

Betty, I don't think that it means that all of the other feelings that surface daily have miraculously disappeared. It is more like the calm of a summer day when there is only the slightest of breezes and all is right with the world. Whatever it is, I think I like it. I hope that I can stay present to this newfound way of thinking about wisdom. I feel like an elder in the best sense of the word.

Oh, my goodness Betty, I am accepting that I know things, lots of things and writing to you has helped me find the beginning of a wisdom that I know will just keep growing. If wisdom is a gift, then I am grateful. If wisdom is something we have to accept, learn about and share, then I am all in. It feels like an early Christmas gift.

Wise Woman,

Me

How do you experience wisdom?

What do you think about wisdom being a gift?

How will you unwrap your own special wisdom?

What Was and What Is

December 18, 2024

Dear Betty,

Getting lids off of bottles, any kind of bottle, seems like nature's cruel way of letting me know that the simplest things in my life are now not so simple. Things that I used to do without even thinking about them now become major projects. Oh Betty, there are still plenty of things that I just do. There is no thinking involved. It reminds me of being in school when we learned what "rote" meant. As I ponder this phenomenon, I realize that what I do most of my days are the things that I do by rote.

The other day I was filling the humidifier. To do this I had to unscrew the cap to the canister that holds the water. It was easy. That simple task brought me to my title for our missive today. I was acutely aware that it was easy. I was certainly capable of completing this task. Betty, I did not have such an easy go of it, though, on another day when I had to take the lid off of a jar. I could not get it off. I finally let it go and waited for someone to walk through my door who might have better luck with it.

Back to the title; "What Was and What Is" speaks to me about how blessed I am to be as strong and healthy as I am. I do have to accept the "what is's" of my life. Those things that I have to admit I need help with or the things that just are. This reminded me of all of the things that I can still have control of. Another lesson for the eighties: realizing that I am really, as the saying goes, "in good shape for the shape I am in." I am still the person I was.

What was is just that, it was and now I accept, or try to accept, the small and large what is that finds clarification in these later in life days.

What will be,

Me

Do you see yourself in the grace of still enjoying what was?

How do you accept the "what is" part of aging?

Things I Wish I Would Have

November 22, 2024

Dear Betty,

How many times do I ask myself, "Why didn't I think about that, or why didn't I do that? Probably way too many. I just sent a Thanksgiving note to someone who I wouldn't call a friend, rather an acquaintance. It was just a short note. I had been thinking about sending it for a day or two. Today I decided to just do it. Now I feel good about making the decision to follow my intuition and I sent the note.

I wonder if I had not sent the note would I have continued to ruminate about or just as usual said, "Oh well." Of course, Betty, this got me thinking about how many times I get a notion to do or say something but I just don't. I talk myself out of it or just simply dismiss the idea and move on. This tells me that I am keeping myself from the gift of being thoughtful. It is not about receiving a reply. What is it then? I think it is trying to be kind, to let someone know that they are worth my time and my words of gratitude or affirmation. I suppose if I am honest/authentic I have to confess that I do like it when I get a response but it is also true Betty that I really don't expect anything.

A busy day ahead. More random thoughts to sift through and thinking that it is one of the things I like about being eighty.

Proud,

Me

What are some of the things that you would put on your list of things you wish you had done or said?

How do you feel when you trust your inner voice and take action?

Naked

November 23, 2024

Dear Betty,

I hardly ever in my life walk around naked. Today I was starting to get ready to take a shower. I was laying out my clothes for the day when I remembered something that I had left in the bathroom. I toddled off in my stage of nakedness. I caught an image of myself in the mirror. All I could see was my head, shoulders, and the space just above my breasts. I thought, "I see all of the parts of my body at one time or another but I sure don't pay much attention to them unless there is an ache or pain. I can tell you that I do not like the changes that occur in an eighty year old body, wrinkles, flab, chunky thighs, you know all of the rest. Betty, this really gave me something to think about.

Could it be that just like I take my body for granted, do I take my inner wellbeing for granted as well? What are the parts of my mind, soul or spirit that I rarely acknowledge? I hope that the lesson here will be attended to by me and I will do a better job of taking inventory of all of the parts of me, even the ones that I am not really happy with now at eighty.

Fully Clothed,

Me

How much attention do you give to caring for your body, all of its parts?

What parts of you do you pay the most attention to and when?

Can any of us only pay attention to the parts of ourselves that are interesting, or exciting or challenging or would it be better to think more holistically?

Message From a Hawk

November 27, 2024

Dear Betty,

I was finding it hard to find words for you today. I am not sure what I am feeling this day before Thanksgiving. It is absolutely quiet here today. It is rather quiet outside as well. The gray winter clouds are not moving, there are no tractors working in the fields and I haven't even heard a random plane flying overhead.

Looking out of my office window I spotted a hawk sitting in the dwarf apple tree. At first, I wasn't sure that it was a hawk but I kept watching or rather looking and sure enough it was a hawk. What does it see I wondered, what is it waiting for or is it waiting? Maybe it is just resting there overlooking its world, my backyard.

Now I hear the very quiet tick, tick of the clock in the sunroom. So, I guess all is not quiet. Time is still being marked, one second at a time. Does the hawk care if time passes? If in fact it is simply resting and observing then I guess it doesn't mind the passing of time. Maybe it is not even observing because that would mean it was doing something, you know Betty, looking around sorting out thoughts about what it sees and on and on. Resting, it is just resting, or at least that is what I choose to believe and it is the lesson that I am still trying to learn. Resting is just resting, being is just being, and all I need to do when I want to emulate the hawk is breath, just breath. Like the hawk, I will move when the spirit moves me into the reality of the day. Grace and peace are with me today, thank you hawk. Happy Thanksgiving.

Breathing,

Me

Do you take the time to listen to the quiet, to just rest?

What is it that makes you uneasy about resting just for resting sake?

What might your lesson be from the story of the hawk?

December

Celebrations at 80

December 1, 2024

Dear Betty,

Do you know that I have been a part of eighty holiday celebrations? Betty, how strange it is to think about that. Of course, I do not have any recollection of the earliest Thanksgiving or Christmases of my life. I am guessing that my first memory of a time that was special was when I was maybe four years old. I received a lovely baby doll from a neighbor of ours whose name was Mrs. Schneider. I am sure that my mom and dad called her by her given name but I was certainly not allowed.

When I think of eighty years of celebrations brings me to such a strange feeling. I don't even quite know how to describe it. There are so many memories of holidays spent with relatives' when I was older, but there are only one or two from my first, second or third celebrations. One I will always remember, well at least I think I will remember, is going to my Aunt Tree and Uncle Joe's house, joining them for midnight mass and then breakfast of the most wonderful sausages one could imagine. Uncle Joe was a butcher and he made the sausages. Aunt Tree made other traditional foods and my mother of course brought her famous cheese torte.

Spending time thinking about this makes me wonder how many holiday gatherings in my eighty years of life have been memorable or nondescript. Each of them seems so important at the time, then they are over and soon we begin to plan for the next year and another celebration. Is this how the story of my life will be told? After all, eighty years is a long time and so many events take place during one's lifetime. Betty, today I like the idea of thinking that I have had the wonder and grace of eighty holiday gatherings. I think I will be more conscious of each one that I am still blessed to celebrate. Somehow the fussing and stress just don't seem as important now, I just want to enjoy all of the celebrations whole-heartedly because I would like to believe that there will be 81, 82, 83 and more for me to still enjoy.

Old Fashioned,

Me

How do you feel about holiday celebrations now?

What makes a celebration special? Was it different when you were younger or is it changing now as an elder?

How has your attitude changed as you have aged?

Stories Tumble Out

December 3, 2024

Dear Betty,

Yesterday, it just occurred to me that I often start my missive to you with yesterday. I guess it is because I am usually writing about what has already happened and because I don't know what is to come. Anyway, granddaughter Tess and daughter Laura came to my house to decorate the tree and the house before our Saint Nik's Supper.

In the process of this undertaking, I found myself relating stories to them. Stories about the old ornaments and where they came from. Stories about the many St. Nik statues I have collected over the years and the reason for each of them. I found myself telling them about the whole bin of garland that they found in the storage area. Tess decided to use most of it all around the house because she said, "If Papa liked it, then we should use it." Use it she did.

To top off the day of holiday magic and storytelling, I got a call from my oldest grandson, Ben. He wanted to know if I would like a quart of soup that he made. "Of course," I said. Well he came over to bring me the soup and by this time I was already donning my warm fuzzy house robe. It was, I think, 8:00 p.m. Again, the conversation found itself happening around more stories tumbling out about the places he remembered visiting with us when he was young. We shared memories of each of them and the time just didn't matter. I expected that he would just drop off the soup and be off and back to his own home but he seemed very comfortable just storytelling, the two of us.

I love these kinds of surprises, the kind that are unexpected and lend themselves to the remembering of stories just too good to lose in the fray. It was a magical moment in this year's holiday season. Fond memories, time standing still, and goodbye hugs.

Keep the stories coming,

Me

How do you feel about surprises?

What are the stories that you want to hold on to?

Pumpkin Bars

December 4, 2024

Dear Betty,

Two days until the family gather here at my home for St. Nik's Supper. I am making soup, bread, and pumpkin bars. I don't know when exactly they got to be a Nana thing but I am commissioned to make them every year. I really don't mind.

Betty, do you think pumpkin bars will be counted as part of my legacy? Why is it that we often remember people because of the things that they cooked or baked or grew in their gardens? Maybe it is because it is once again the simple things in life that at times become the most meaningful.

I recently found this writing and today I think it is so relevant. I only hope that I can remember its message and add it to my to-do list. Here it is:

"The sweetest treasures were always here – in honest words, in the courage to stay soft, in finding peace between storms. After all my searching, all my longing for more, I finally understand. The most precious things are these simple moments that string our days together, these ordinary breaths between thunder. How strange that what I needed most was already here, waiting in the spaces between heartbeats."

Quiet Treasures by Etheric Echoes

I guess Betty, that along with the simple moments I might add the aromas wafting from the kitchen at these holidays. The warm soup mom had on the stove in the dark days of winter and the hope that springs from the ongoing planting of the annual garden. It is because it is the "simple moments that string our days together."

Out of the oven,

Me

What are the simple treasures that you hope will become part of your legacy?

How do you feel about carrying on traditions like baking pumpkin bars? Or whatever makes you feel warm and cozy?

Small

December 6, 2024

Dear Betty,

Although there were a few family members missing last night at our St. Nik's Supper, the house was still full of youthful energy. The story of St. Nik was shared. The tree lights fascinated the little ones and the gold coin candies were a hit.

Even though Betty, I know how important it is to keep family traditions alive, I wonder how long this one will endure. I was exhausted by the end of the evening. All morning I have been trying to name my feelings of last night and this morning. I am not quite there yet.

Last night amidst all of the various conversations, and the moms trying to wrangle their kids, I found myself feeling rather small. Not in the physical sense but more like almost invisible. I am doing my best to enjoy the youngers and to engage with my children and grandchildren but sometimes it is difficult. I have come to really appreciate being with those in the realm of an age I can relate too.

So, Betty, another year to count as a well-worn tradition. I will let you know if I will continue it next year. I have a whole year to think about it and then I will be eighty-one.

Happy St. Nik's,

Me

What family traditions do you think you have to hold on to?

How do you feel when you are in the midst of large gatherings that seem a bit chaotic?

What counts as a fun and successful gathering in your book?

Up-Ended

December 9, 2024

Dear Betty,

I thought that I had a good understanding of the word upended. The feeling of being turned upside down seemed to fit for me today. Then, as usual, Betty, I decided to look up the definition and for the first time I chose the definition given by AI. Now I am feeling like I am really with it or as my grandchildren would say, "fire."

"Upended life" means a life that has been drastically turned upside down, completely disrupted, or significantly altered, often due to a major event or change that has thrown everything into disarray; essentially, it signifies a life that is no longer in its usual state and is facing significant upheaval.

This feeling of upendedness seems to suit me today. As I managed to host St. Nik's supper and then followed the next day with Christmas shopping, I found myself stuck in the question, "What does it all mean now at eighty?" I have told stories about our various family traditions, the old ornaments on the tree, and the food that we share. Still, I am feeling a bit upside down, my life is no longer in its usual state, why Betty? Well, I am sure that part of the issue is Don's absence. I am also trying to come to grips with the fact that I have celebrated eighty Christmases. Of course, I do not have any memory of those early years, the first five probably. How many of the others can I say I was truly present for, not just going through the motions? So many things about holidays seem to be upended, turned around, and disrupted.

Seems to me Betty, that I have plenty to sort out when it comes to my feelings around this holiday season. What should I do to set myself upright again?

Searching,

Me

What makes you feel upended?

How do you set yourself upright again?

How many meaningful Christmases have you enjoyed?

Usual

December 11, 2024

Dear Betty.

Usual. Today I think that it is the best word to describe how I am feeling Betty. I am trying to convince myself that I am enjoying this holiday season but each day, although there are holiday-like things I could be doing, I am happy to just be doing the usual.

I enjoy the spirit of Christmas, or honestly I used to, now it kind of feels like the same old, same old. I sound like a grinch don't I Betty? Well, I am trying to be authentic, real about my feelings. Should I try to figure out why I am feeling like such a downer or should I just put one foot in front of the other and get through the season?

Now I have a tear that has escaped out of my eye and it is rolling down my cheek. This is not a sad tear but rather one caused by the winter cold that I have managed to succumb to. It is not a bad metaphor for how I am feeling, though. A little out of control and waiting to be caught in something soft and comforting. Wow, Betty, what exactly am I trying to say to you today?

Maybe I want to experience something that is not usual but unusual, exciting, childlike and maybe I need to acknowledge that I miss Don and the way he celebrated the season of Christmas. For him it was certainly not usual. He was present to all of it, especially the parts that involved his grandchildren. So, Betty, I will never have the same enthusiasm that he had but I can certainly stop feeling grumpy about the usual and I can create a bit of the unusual by striving to be present to each day and at least a little of the holiday spirit.

Does the journey of eighty have to only be usual? I think not!

Stretching my holiday muscle,

Me

Do you think that it is important to be present to the unusual?

What brings you comfort in these winter days?

How do you feel about entering into the holiday spirit?

Soon 81

December 14, 2024

Dear Betty,

When do we know when something is finished? It is easy when baking bread, simply insert a kitchen thermometer, and make sure it is at the right degree. Life is not as easy to gauge.

Next month I will celebrate my eighty-first birthday. Where did this year of eighty go? This is a phrase we hear often when we are referencing time. Oh, my, the party is over, it is time to go. Where did the time go? You get the picture don't you Betty?

For these next few days until the calendar turns its page and a new year arrives, I will try to look back at this year of eighty. What lessons have I learned, what questions do I still have? How different am I today than I was almost a year ago? I wonder if this will be a productive thing to do or should I just try to be present in each day and accept them as they come? Since writing to you has never been contrived or has not had a great plan, I will continue to simply try to get in touch with my thoughts and feelings on any given day. I will share them with you because writing to you is a good exercise that keeps me grounded or centered or whatever the catch phrase is for being authentic these days.

Soon 81,

Me

Do you think much about impending birthdays?

What might be the lessons that you have learned this past year?

How will you celebrate another year or will you?

Feeling AWE

December 21, 2024

Dear Betty,

Sometimes you just have to let yourself be amazed or awestruck. I allowed this to happen to me the other day when I opened the blind in my bedroom and saw that mother nature had gifted us with a fresh new first time this winter snow.

How beautiful it was. The trees decked out in fluffy glistening snow. The dried and brown hydrangeas out of my sun room window were wearing caps of sparkling white.

I know that it will not last.

How does this experience relate to my exploration of my life at eighty? The obvious thought is some things just don't last. Change is difficult at best, but at eighty it could be the worst.

I think it is all in how I decide to view each day and I hope that I am going to continue to be aware of the feeling of amazement or being awestruck. These fleeting moments are what make my days worth the effort that it takes to open the blinds and notice.

Letting the view in,

Me

What makes you awestruck?

How do you hold on to the feeling of awe?

Holidays at 80

December 25, 2024

Dear Betty,

The family gathered and as usual there was laughter, excitement, the warm welcoming smell of things cooking on the stove. There was also chaos, drama and unfortunately the forgetting of some of the long-held traditions.

Betty, I don't want to spoil your holiday but I have to tell you that this year's festivities are finding me sad and too emotional for my liking. Why is this happening, I ask myself? I remember getting through the holidays with little emotion last year. Is it because I have had a whole year to process my loss? Is it because I am alone? Maybe I have just become too complacent about it all now in my eightieth year?

Yes, I did enjoy watching the little ones all dressed up in their special clothes and flitting from one new toy to another. Ah, the joy of being a little one. Now I am thinking that perhaps I am not the only one feeling a bit downhearted. After all, I am not the only one who has suffered loss. The entire family is in many ways missing his presence. Although I am the oldest, others are not far behind.

Soon it will be a new year and we will continue to find our way.

81 soon,

Me

How do you feel about experiencing times when all is not well?

What do you do to acknowledge the reality of a holiday that holds so many feelings?

Are you planning for a new year or not ready for what is new as yet?

Winter Fog

December 26, 2024

Dear Betty,

It was supposed to lift. That is what the weather forecasters said. Well Betty, it is midday now and it is still foggy. It is giving me a good metaphor for how I am feeling today. I heard that fog is just low-hanging clouds, sometimes it touches the ground. It takes longer for it to dissipate in the cold days of winter.

Well Betty, you can see where I am going with this, can't you? More and more I have come to grips with understanding that this is in fact the winter of my life. Now that I am at the end of my eightieth year, I look out across winter fields at the fog. I think that although I have learned much about my aging process this year, the fog of understanding is still a bit heavy at times.

Sunny days do seem to help me see more clearly. In other seasons of foggy mornings when I have enjoyed the warmth of the sun and the fog lifts, I sense a certain peace of mind. Things that were puzzling seem to find their way to fitting together. Today is not one of them. Those seasons are long gone. Yes Betty, there are sunny winter days but I find that days like today encourage me to appreciate the idea that I still have much to learn and experience as a wise woman in her eightieth decade and in the winter of her life. Today the fog is not worrisome to me because I know that when it begins to clear it will leave a sparkling, glittering presence on the trees and bushes just outside of my window. I have much to look forward to, don't you think?

Out of the fog,

Me

What does the metaphor of a foggy day mean to you?

How do you feel about spending a day in the fog?

How have you experienced foggy days in the past?

Fog Continued

December 30, 2024

Dear Betty,

Days and days of fog have given me so many more thoughts and feelings about ending my eightieth year. Some of the foggy days have been so dark and dank and dense that I could hardly see past where the backyard ends and the first pasture begins. Thus, I am reminded that there have been many times when I have not felt that I understood anything about this life stage. Then there are the days when, although it's still relatively dark by the middle of the day, the fog lifts. I can see far into the back forty. I think that these are the times when I am willing to take the opportunity to stop and think about why I was feeling like I was in a fog, not sure where I was or where I was going.

Finally, today the sun is finally shining. "Ah ha" I said to myself, and then just as I was feeling proud of myself for recognizing how bright the world seemed I saw way out there in the distance a veil of fog. Betty, I think it was taunting me. It was pronouncing itself and reminding that there will always be somethings that will never be clear. Some things about my continuing years in the eighties I will just have to accept without clarity. However, just by acknowledging this I see that I have just had a realization. At times lying just past the bright shiny clarity of a blue sky day there may still be uncertainty, a veil of fog offering an opportunity for still more. Betty, I like "more" don't you?

Betty, don't you just love metaphors? "Me thinks" that I will embrace fog now because it has become part of my consciousness. It is another friend that has helped me explore the meaning or maybe the message of my reality I call my "now". Together Betty, we will continue to look for more messages brought to us by the unbelievable out there that surrounds us.

A toast to fog,

Me

What helps you define your life journey at this time of your life?

How do you feel about exploring your experiences of foggy days?

Do you find this kind of exploration helpful in your understanding of your "now"?

Reality Check Again

December 31, 2024

Dear Betty,

I walked into the holiday fully prepared to be present, to enjoy all of the festivities. What a surprise lay ahead of me. I started feeling under the weather at Thanksgiving and continued feeling that was off and on until New Years Eve when the head cold I had been warding off returned in full force.

Sometimes I guess I just need a reality check. I am not as young as I used to be, nor do I have the same immune system that I have been blessed with for most of my life.

Well, Betty, I am not going to go on with this sad story. I am going to say that since I have not had a holiday season quite like this for some years, it was a reminder that I have much to be grateful for health wise. I am usually pretty darn healthy. This past month has brought me to the acceptance that I will, or I might have more times of feeling poorly than not. So many things pop up at this stage of life that I am sure I would be happy to ignore but then Betty, remember that thing I have about being authentic? Well here we go!

Keeping it real,

Me

What gives you pause, or causes you to have a reality check?

How do these times make you feel?

January

Finding Words

January 3, 2025

Dear Betty,

Words. In the early days of writing to you about my eightieth year it occurs to me that I wrote a lot about words. About exploring the meaning of words, and about how certain words helped me describe what I was either feeling or experiencing on any given day.

Now, as we can count down the days to my next birthday, my eighty-first, I notice that I have not been as engaged with words as I was in the beginning. So, for the next few days I may write to you, again through the lens of words.

More. Today the word more comes to mind. As I sit here today looking out of my window and wishing that I might see something out there that will help me describe today. The sky is streaked with various shades of blue, blue gray, white and just a hint of a glow from the sunshine that is hidden behind the far away clouds. I want more. More than just a streak of sunlight across my desk, more than the faded blue and ribbons of white.

I guess Betty, I have found the metaphor that I was looking for. Just as I want more color in my sky, more sunlight across my desk and clear bright white of understanding, I want more. More has been a gift that I can identify now as having given me more understanding, more awareness, more lessons about my inner and outer self than I had at the beginning of this monumental year. Still, Betty, I believe that there is even more to come if I stay open to the process of more. By this I mean that just when I think I have learned each lesson there is a knock at my inner door asking me to invite in still more. Answering the door usually means enjoying the experience of appreciation. Who can't be more appreciative these days?

Practicing more,

Me

How do you experience "more" in your life?

What do you think about the idea of practicing the process of more?

How does it feel to you when you realize another "something" to be appreciative about?

Talking Mad

January 8, 2025

Dear Betty,

Have you ever thought much about the tone of voice that you hear when someone wants to impart an important message? I hadn't either Betty. The other day however, I heard a woman on a news show addressing a committee of some sort.

Wow, I thought, she sounds really upset. As I continued to listen I was more intent on hearing the sound of her voice than in what she was talking about. I still don't remember what her angst was about. What I do know is that I named her address to the committee "mad talking."

Mad talking, I thought, now here is another thing that I can try to notice as I listen to the world around me. Does it make others listen to us more intently if we are loud? What about having an angry note in our voice? If we stop any inflection at all, will we be able to make our point? Betty, you know that I have from time to time raised my voice, maybe even slapped my hand down on a table or counter to illustrate my feeling at any given time.

I wonder if we might be more likely to get the result we want if we lower the tone of our voice, try to, what is that old saying? Walk gently and carry a big stick. Perhaps I would be better at being listened to if I practiced being clear about what I was presenting, trying to stay even spoken and stop mad talking.

Finally, Betty, I do think we would live in a dull and sterile world if we didn't use something like our voice to make a point or to let another know that we were trying to express a feeling. No matter what the feeling might be.

Gentle talking,

Me

What have been your experiences of mad talking?

Do you think that using one's voice is helpful in letting others know how we are feeling?

Counting

January 10, 2025

Dear Betty,

Only eight more days to my eighty-first birthday. Over and over again we say, "how can it be, a whole year gone by, seemed like yesterday." Still, it is the way of our lives. Time passes and we move on.

In just four days our collection of letters will be published and out there in the big wide world for all to read. I really do hope Betty that our letters are helpful to others who are asking the questions that we asked. What do we do when we reach our "golden" years? I am not sure that we have answered the "what do we do" part of that question but I feel that I have a deeper understanding of who I am and what this past year meant to me.

Now I think that I need to go back over the letters of the past year and try to find a concrete way to come to an awareness of the lessons I have learned. I will also find that I am sure that there are more questions and although I might acknowledge the lessons, I have not fully addressed how to put them into practice.

What will we explore next Betty? Who knows?

Counting days to another monumental birthday,

Me

Do you find yourself counting down the days? To what, with whom?

What is your plan for entering another year of life on planet earth?

How do you feel about this year's birthday?

Amazed

January 11, 2025

Dear Betty,

Just because I am not very patient about some things, I went to the Amazon website and searched for our book. I searched for "Letters to Betty by Mary Bub." Then Betty, I was overwhelmed with emotion. I was stunned and amazed when I saw the image of our book right there on my screen. Yes, I knew it was coming but I only decided to look for it on a whim. Maybe wanting it to be there, maybe hoping it would be, maybe not believing that this whole journey has happened.

What an adventure publishing a book is. Who would have thought that I would be a published author? You know who would believe it? Don. I so wish that he was here to enjoy the fruit of our life together.

I wish that I could say that I had this dream. That I always wanted to write a book. I cannot say that. I can say that I followed my intuition, the drive that I have always had to follow the multi-colored road to wherever it leads. So, my intention was not about a fulfilled dream. Selfishly my intent was to find a way to process my grief after losing Don and I can honestly say that it was to help others through their times of loss.

I know that this sounds a bit puffed up, full of ego, but I hope that you will not read it that way Betty. Being a storyteller has been one piece of the puzzle that is me and if even one person gets solace from our letters, then I hope that they catch the story as it was offered.

Amazed,

Me

What amazes you?

What might you choose as your intent for your inner listening?

How will you celebrate your amazement?

Be Holy

January 13, 2025

Dear Betty,

Be holy. Yesterday I heard a song that offered the invitation to take time to be holy. Of course, you know Betty that I would have to define what being holy meant for me. After looking at many definitions I have come to think that for me the word holy is an adjective. It is something used to make a strong statement.

Some examples might be "holy cow" or "holy Christmas". How does this translate into my being holy? Yes, there are many examples of how various faiths describe being holy. I, being a simple person or at least one who needs to distill things down to a place I can relate, take it to mean that I need to try to be whatever I think it is to be holy.

Here is what I think Betty. I think that if I am going to be holy, I need to be kind and caring, loving and forgiving, aware of my stance in my life today. Simply, I will have to try to be better tomorrow than I am today. Contrary to much of what we hear from our culture's gurus about self-assurance or holistic wellness, I do think that for myself, I do think that there is more that I can be, do, and learn.

Trying to be holy,

Me

Do you take time or give thoughts to being holy?

What does being holy mean to you?

How would you define the invitation to be holy?

Who Knew?

January 15, 2025

Dear Betty,

Today is my daughter Christy's birthday. She is 60 years old today. When I think about her today, I see her at so many birthdays. I see her as a little girl who was always ready to protect her older sister. I see her as a teenager experiencing all of the joy and heartbreak, the challenges and the growing up. I see her on her wedding day, beautiful and happy. I remember how sad I was when she left for Japan with her new husband. I see her with her newborn children and remember her with the same protective spirit that she had when she was little.

Who knew that today we would be celebrating a milestone birthday with her on the same day that our letters would reach the bestseller list at Amazon? I can hardly believe that all of the things that have come together that add another dimension to our lives.

Who knew that there would even be a book, much less one that would appear on my computer screen? Who knew that we would receive so many kind and thoughtful comments about our work together Betty?

I feel like a proud mom who needs to give Christy's day due notice. I feel like a youngster excited about a new chapter in my own life appearing when I thought that my service days were over. Betty, do you think that it is OK to celebrate both of these things? I do.

Deep down knowing,

Me

What do you think about times when you face a dichotomy?

How do you feel about the "who knew" times in your own experience?

Celebrate the wonder of "who knew" moments.

Shoes

January 16, 2025

Dear Betty,

The other day I was getting dressed to go to a funeral. I went into my closet to get my shoes and realized that I automatically choose my tennis shoes. Are they still called tennis shoes? I don't know. Aren't they sometimes just referred to by the company name or as walking or running shoes?

What I really noticed however, as I laced up my whatever shoes was a feeling that yet another milestone was happening right in that moment. I thought, "I have just entered the tennis shoe club." Is this another rite of passage for us olders?

I have enjoyed many shoes in my footwear lifetime. Oh, the days when high heels meant that I had become a young woman. I also enjoyed the extra benefit of those wondrous heels making me at least one inch taller. Then there were the days of the western boots that were a must while helping my farming uncle at the state fair. Saddle shoes had nothing to do with saddles. I wonder Betty why they were called saddle shoes? They were flat and black and white and needed regular polishing. The pattern leather shoes were for special occasions or Sundays but left behind when I graduated to those "high heels."

There were probably others but my point here Betty is that most days now, even when I am wearing a dress or going to church, it is the tennis shoe that wins the contest. At 81 years young I am proud to say that I am a member of the Tennis Shoe Club, walking and cavorting with my similarly footed friends and companions.

Walk on,

Me

Eighty-One

January 18, 2025

Dear Betty,

The year of eighty is over. We did it Betty! I don't feel any different than I did when I went to bed last night. However, I am happy to say that during our year of eighty I was able to learn about the many facets of life in my elder years.

I continue to process the grief that I know will never leave me. I am proud to say that by sharing the journey I have heard that others have been aided to follow their own paths.

You know Betty that my ambition for many of my eightieth years has been to become authentic, wise, and eccentric. I do feel that I am as authentic in myself and in my relationships with others as I can be. I catch glimpses of my own wisdom from time to time and for this I am grateful as it affirms the work. I have tried to pursue it for most of my adult life. Finally, I am going to work on the eccentric bit. I am not really sure why this is so appealing to me, so it seems that exploring its meaning will be a worthwhile time of learning and more growing into whatever it is that I am supposed to become.

Authentic Wise Eccentric = AWE

I don't know when I will be writing to you again but I am fairly sure that it will happen.

Another year another journey,

Me

Afterword

I feel that this poem explains succinctly the journey that I have pursued in my eightieth year. My hope is that it will carry me well into the next year and beyond. I want to experience the throb of amazement, the ping and swell of authentic and wise moments. I want to be attentive to my own eccentric self, bless my soul and yours as well. I want to celebrate the AWE.

"Ten Times A Day" by poet Mary Oliver

Ten times a day

Something happens to me

Like this – some

Strengthening throb of amazement

Some good sweet empathic ping and swell.

This is the first, the wildest and the wisest thing I know.

That the soul exists and is built entirely out of attentiveness.

Mary Bub is a grassroots activist, social innovator, author, artist, and photographer. She is the co-founder, past president, and currently an advisor of Wisconsin Rural Women's Initiative, a nonprofit organization that provides on-site grassroots programs to individual women and organizations through a Gathering Circle process promoting personal development, transformation, and systemic change. She is the winner of the Social Innovation Prize in Wisconsin for 2008, A Purpose Prize Fellow with Civic Ventures, a recipient of the Feminarian Award, and a winner of Wisconsin's Top Rural Development Initiatives. In addition to *Letters to Betty at 80*, Mary is the author of *Letters to Betty, And So It Goes A Woman in My Soul, The Angel of the Wood,* and *This is No Merry Widow's Story.*

Mary is a widow, mother, grandmother, great-grandmother, friend, facilitator of a small circle of Kindreds, and Officiant of Memorial Services. She lives on MoonStar Farm with her dog York and cat Liza.

www.marybubauthor.com

www.ingramcontent.com/pod-product-compliance
Lightning Source LLC
Chambersburg PA
CBHW051455030726
47592CB00006B/1932